ETA

ESTHER-MATED TIME OF ARRIVAL

12 MONTH DEVOTIONAL AND JOURNAL

TIFFANY BUCKNER

E.T.A.
Esther-mated Time of Arrival
Tiffany Buckner

©2020, Tiffany Buckner
www.tiffanybuckner.com
info@anointedfire.com

PUBLISHED BY ANOINTED FIRE HOUSE

COVER DESIGN BY ANOINTED FIRE HOUSE

PHOTO BY: BRAND YOU BRAND NU

ISBN: 978-1-7354654-3-2

This book contains material protected under International and Federal Copyright Laws and Treaties. Any unauthorized reprint or use of this material is prohibited. No part of this book may be reproduced or transmitted in any form or by any means, electronic or mechanical, including photocopying, recording, or by any information storage and retrieval system without express written permission from the author/publisher. For permission requests, write to the publisher, at "Attention: Permissions Coordinator," at the address below:
Tiffany Buckner
info@anointedfire.com

Although the author and publisher have made every effort to ensure that the information in this book was correct at press time, the author and publisher do not assume and hereby disclaim any liability to any party for any loss, damage, or disruption caused by errors or omissions, whether such errors or omissions result from negligence, accident, or any other cause.

This book is not intended as a substitute for the medical advice of physicians. The reader should regularly consult a physician in matters relating to his/her health and particularly with respect to any symptoms that may require diagnosis or medical attention.

Scripture quotations marked ESV are taken from The Holy Bible, English Standard Version®. English Standard Version are registered trademarks of Crossway®.

For information about special discounts available for bulk purchases, sales promotions, fund-raising and educational needs, contact Anointed Fire House (Sales) at info@anointedfire.com

This is your Esther tracking device. The goal of this tracker is to track and trace your deficiencies and to document your growth. Understand this—growth is not incidental, it is always intentional, meaning, you have to intentionally, strategically and consistently study and apply the Word of God until it becomes a habit.

Be transparent and be truthful, remembering that your mentor cannot coach what he/she cannot see. If you hide it, it's because you want to keep it or because guilt and shame have muzzled you.

Trace	find or discover by investigation	This deals with your history
Track	follow the course or trail of (someone or something), typically in order to find them or note their location at various points.	This deals with your present and your future
Definitions taken from Google		

All of your issues have footprints.
This is why they have to be traced and they have to be tracked.

Table of Contents

Introduction..IX
Profile of an Esther...XI
   Your Story..XIII
   Generational Curse Tracker..XIX
      Paternal...XXIII
      Maternal..XXV
How to Use This Manual..XXVII

Month One

From Hardship to Leadership..1
   Esther Tracer..5
   Esther's Trail..6
   Prayer Closet...7
   Challenge of the Month..7
   Esther's Edict...7
   Esther Tracker..8

Month Two

Break the Curse..19
   Esther Tracer..25
   Esther's Trail..26
   Prayer Closet...27
   Challenge of the Month..27
   Esther's Edict...27
   Esther Tracker..28

Month Three

Fitting into Your Crown..39
   Esther Tracer..45
   Esther's Trail..46
   Prayer Closet...47
   Challenge of the Month..47
   Esther's Edict...47
   Esther Tracker..48

Month Four

The Power of Submission...59
   Esther Tracer..65
   Esther's Trail..66
   Prayer Closet...67
   Challenge of the Month..67

    Esther's Edict...67
    Esther Tracker...68

Month Five

    The Beauty of Holiness..79
    Esther Tracer...85
    Esther's Trail..86
    Prayer Closet..87
    Challenge of the Month..87
    Esther's Edict...87
    Esther Tracker...88

Month Six

    Forgive Them and Move On..99
    Esther Tracer...105
    Esther's Trail..106
    Prayer Closet..107
    Challenge of the Month..107
    Esther's Edict...107
    Esther Tracker...108

Month Seven

    Make Fear Serve You...119
    Esther Tracer...125
    Esther's Trail..126
    Prayer Closet..127
    Challenge of the Month..127
    Esther's Edict...127
    Esther Tracker...128

Month Eight

    Love Your Enemies..139
    Esther Tracer...145
    Esther's Trail..146
    Prayer Closet..147
    Challenge of the Month..147
    Esther's Edict...147
    Esther Tracker...148

Month Nine

    Conquer, but Don't Forget to Heal...159
    Esther Tracer...166
    Esther's Trail..167
    Prayer Closet..168

- CHALLENGE OF THE MONTH...............168
- ESTHER'S EDICT...............168
- ESTHER TRACKER...............169

Month Ten

The Great Falling Away...............181
- ESTHER TRACKER...............186
- ESTHER'S TRAIL...............187
- PRAYER CLOSET...............188
- CHALLENGE OF THE MONTH...............188
- ESTHER'S EDICT...............188
- ESTHER TRACKER...............189

Month Eleven

You're a Queen, Not a Concubine...............201
- ESTHER TRACKER...............207
- ESTHER'S TRAIL...............208
- PRAYER CLOSET...............209
- CHALLENGE OF THE MONTH...............209
- ESTHER'S EDICT...............209
- ESTHER TRACKER...............210

Month Twelve

Possess the Promise...............221
- ESTHER TRACKER...............227
- ESTHER'S TRAIL...............228
- PRAYER CLOSET...............229
- CHALLENGE OF THE MONTH...............229
- ESTHER'S EDICT...............229
- ESTHER TRACKER...............230

Personal Constitution...............241

How to Use the Constitution...............243
- DATES AND DEFINITIONS...............244
- UNDERSTANDING LEGALITIES...............246
- SELF-GOVERNANCE...............250
  - ARTICLE I
- FAMILIAL RELATIONSHIPS...............251
  - ARTICLE II
- PLATONIC RELATIONSHIPS...............253
  - ARTICLE III
- ROMANTIC RELATIONSHIPS...............255
  - ARTICLE IV
- MONEY MATTERS...............257

ARTICLE V.
PEER/PROFESSIONAL RELATIONSHIPS...259
ARTICLE VI.
OTHER RELATIONSHIPS..261
ARTICLE VII.

INTRODUCTION

E.T.A. (Esther-mated Time of Arrival) was initially being designed as a tool for the students of Esther Prep University (a division of Anointed Fire). Nevertheless, it developed into a tool that the author believed most women could benefit from, so she decided to make it available to the public.

The purpose of E.T.A. is to help women to mature into the roles that they so earnestly desire to fill and, of course, the roles they are called to fill. This is an accountability tool that will allow you to monitor your movements over a span of twelve months. Additionally, you will find tips, challenges and revelations that will help to encourage, edify and push you towards your destiny.

You will find space to document your movements and journal about your feelings, fears and victories, and much more. This devotional/journal was inspired by Esther 2:12.

ESTHER 2:12

Now when the turn came for each young woman to go in to King Ahasuerus, after being twelve months under the regulations for the women, since this was the regular period of their beautifying, six months with oil of myrrh and six months with spices and ointments for women.

And please note that while King Ahasuerus (also known as King Xerxes) was a pagan king and womanizer, the reason God sent Esther to serve as his wife was so that He could use her to rescue the Jews. Nevertheless, He later instructed us to not be unequally yoked with unbelievers. He wasn't being hypocritical, He was simply communicating a message to us—Esther was designed, broken and developed to serve alongside a pagan king because she had an assignment that was bigger than herself; you were designed to serve alongside a Godly man because you have an assignment that's bigger than yourself. Yes, God still uses and prepares His daughters to serve in powerful roles, however, most women don't graduate from the ungodly mindsets that keep them enslaved to the elements of this world. Consequently, they spend their lives serving as concubines (girlfriends) to a bunch of random men, never really knowing what it's like to be loved, truly appreciated, protected, provided for and led. This tool was created to help women to break those vicious cycles and finally take their places as the Queens they are designed to become.

Profile of an Esther

ALL ABOUT YOU

Your Name	
Your Nickname	
Birth Date	
Parents' Names	
Children's Names	
Birth City and State	
Current City and State	
Degree	
Occupation	
Hobbies	
Aspirations	

SPIRITUALITY

Your Church's Name	
Your Pastor	
Religious Denomination	
Your Title (License/Ordination)	
Your Beliefs	

Your Story

Exodus 13:3

And Moses said unto the people, Remember this day, in which ye came out from Egypt, out of the house of bondage; for by strength of hand the LORD brought you out from this place: there shall no leavened bread be eaten.

Remember (verb): have in or be able to bring to one's mind an awareness of (someone or something that one has seen, known, or experienced in the past).
Definition taken from Google's Online Dictionary

Use this section to journal about the most life-changing events of your life, including traumatic and exciting events. The goal of this is for you to see where you've come from so that whenever you arrive at your destination, you will see how far God has brought you. Additionally, this tool may serve as a guide for your children, grandchildren and descendants, allowing them to see what you had to do to break generational curses and establish generational blessings.
(See example below.)

Date, Year or Age	Event Type	Event Details
14 years old	Traumatic	Abandoned by father

Does this event still affect you, and if so, how?
Yes, it's still hard for me to trust men or people in authority.

Date, Year or Age	Event Type	Event Details

Does this event still affect you, and if so, how?

Date, Year or Age	Event Type	Event Details

Does this event still affect you, and if so, how?

Date, Year or Age	Event Type	Event Details

Does this event still affect you, and if so, how?

Date, Year or Age	Event Type	Event Details

Does this event still affect you, and if so, how?

Date, Year or Age	Event Type	Event Details

Does this event still affect you, and if so, how?

Date, Year or Age	Event Type	Event Details

Does this event still affect you, and if so, how?

Date, Year or Age	Event Type	Event Details

Does this event still affect you, and if so, how?

Date, Year or Age	Event Type	Event Details

Does this event still affect you, and if so, how?

Date, Year or Age	Event Type	Event Details

Does this event still affect you, and if so, how?

Date, Year or Age	Event Type	Event Details

Does this event still affect you, and if so, how?

Generational Curse Tracker

Numbers 14:18

The LORD is longsuffering, and of great mercy, forgiving iniquity and transgression, and by no means clearing the guilty, visiting the iniquity of the fathers upon the children unto the third and fourth generation.

Exodus 20:5-6

Thou shalt not bow down thyself to them, nor serve them: for I the LORD thy God am a jealous God, visiting the iniquity of the fathers upon the children unto the third and fourth generation of them that hate me; and shewing mercy unto thousands of them that love me, and keep my commandments.

Ezekiel 18:19-20

Yet say ye, Why? Doth not the son bear the iniquity of the father? When the son hath done that which is lawful and right, and hath kept all my statutes, and hath done them, he shall surely live. The soul that sinneth, it shall die. The son shall not bear the iniquity of the father, neither shall the father bear the iniquity of the son: the righteousness of the righteous shall be upon him, and the wickedness of the wicked shall be upon him.

The word "generational" is built of two very familiar words:
1. Gene: (*in informal use*) a unit of heredity which is transferred from a parent to offspring and is held to determine some characteristic of the offspring.
2. Rational: involving only multiplication, division, addition, and subtraction and only a finite number of times.

First, let's address the obvious. It would appear that while Numbers 14:18 and Exodus 20:5-6 seem to echo one other, Ezekiel 18 seems to contradict them both. In truth, they don't contradict one another; you just have to thoroughly examine the text. God said that He would "visit" the iniquity of the fathers, not place them upon the children. Does this then dispel the concept of generational curses? No, it doesn't. A generational curse is a predisposition to particular pattern of thoughts which, of course, lead to a particular pattern of decisions, all of which lead to a common result. It's circling the same mountain, hoping that you'll arrive at a different destination. For example, think of diseases like diabetes and high blood pressure. While both are known to travel from one generation to the next, the truth of the matter is, a child will not automatically "inherit" these diseases; instead, the child "inherits" the eating patterns (learned behaviors) of the parents, after all, parents can only teach their children what they know. Generational curses fall under or abide by this same concept. Here are two facts to consider:

1. Systems (Mindsets): Sons and daughters learn from their parents, so if one or both parents, for example, are bound by a victim's mentality and relies on the government for their sustenance, this mindset is passed down to the children because the children have never witnessed their parents enduring the pressures associated with being productive. This causes the children to lack long-suffering and to be extremely emotional and dependent. Additionally, the children will see themselves as victims, and this line of reasoning gives way to entitlement. This is the system of a generational curse. Another example of the systematic destruction of a bloodline occurs when children don't get what they need to become emotionally healthy adults. For example, a father abandons his wife and children, causing the children to deal with the traumas of abandonment and rejection. Without the presence of a father, many children begin to rebel in an attempt to get his attention or draw attention from others to their pain-laced anger. This starts a domino effect of destruction that follows them from childhood to adulthood, and it eventually crosses over into the next generation, then the next; that is, until someone confronts and dismantles it.

2. Spirits: Unclean spirits do travel from one generation to the next, but God didn't send them to the people. They entered in through agreements; for example, a young woman in 1935 finds herself petrified at the idea of losing her husband. The couple has six children, with another child on the way. The husband starts having an affair with a woman who lives around the corner from the couple. He becomes verbally, mentally and physically abusive towards his wife and children. The wife decides to leave him, but her parents and family members send her back home, blaming her for the chaos in her marriage. "Fix yourself up sometimes!" they shout. "If you were taking care of him at home, he wouldn't be doing the things he's doing!" they scream, echoing the sentiments of his pestering mistress. *(Believe it or not, this was very common back then!)* The man may be dealing with a generational stronghold of lust and divorce, but the enemy has another plan because Satan thinks in generations. At the time, women made four times less money than men, so it was impossible for them to provide for themselves alone, so they definitely could not provide for their children by themselves. With no support from family, little to no income of her own and almost seven mouths to feed, the woman finally sits down and listens to her friend who tells her about a "madam" who lives (and works) from her home. The

madam, of course, is a witch who says that the other woman has "roots" on the husband, thus explaining his erratic behavior. She claims that she can break the curse. Desperate, the wife reaches into her purse and pulls out the money she's been saving and hiding from her husband. What she doesn't know is that she's just entered a contractual agreement with the kingdom of darkness and those spirits will travel for and affect/attack a certain number of generations until the agreement expires, the devil collects his wages (the death, perversion and bondage of so many souls) or someone wises up and breaks the curse.

So when God said that He would "visit" the sins of the fathers upon the sons, He wasn't saying that He would punish the sons for what their fathers did. He was simply saying that He would address these sins if and when they manifested themselves generation after generation. And get this, they always manifest!

Most, if not all, generational curses started with dishonor. For example, a woman bears the surname of her paternal father until another man comes along and marries her. She then takes on his surname. Traditionally, men had to go through the fathers to get to the daughters, but cultural shifts, man-made traditions and the normalization of fornication have caused dishonor to become commonplace. And of course, dishonor isn't just limited to sexual immorality. If a man owed a debt to another man, and he refused to pay that debt, he was (and is) operating in dishonor. If a child rebels against his or her parents, that child is operating in dishonor. If a man or woman commits adultery, that individual (and the mister or mistress) is operating in dishonor. Remember this rule—bound people hate boundaries. Anyone who violates a God-established or man-established boundary has operated in dishonor. A curse is the response to the dishonor. And please note that the word "curse" means that God has withdrawn or withheld His blessing from a mindset or event. This is why you personally can't be cursed, but a mindset can be.

With this noted, you can use the Generational Curse Tracker to trace dishonor in your family, and be sure to repent of the deed and renounce it. Repenting doesn't mean that you're acknowledging guilt on your end; it simply means that you are turning back around to follow Christ, whereas traditionally, your family had been heading in the wrong direction in a particular arena (family, finances, marriage, etc.). Of course, I listed an example for you to start with.

Please note that in some families, it is considered disrespectful or dishonorable to mention the dark things that took place in that family. Be free from that man-made tradition. Healing and deliverance start when you take what's in the dark (secrets) and bring them to the light (God). "This then is the message which we have heard of him, and declare unto you, that God is light, and in him is no darkness at all" (1 John 1:5).

EXAMPLE

Generations	Surnames	Generational Issue/ Event
Your Surname	Buckner	Divorce (2x)
Father's Surname	Buckner	Divorce (2x)
Grandfather's Surname	Buckner	Divorce (1x) Left wife and abandoned children after wife's passing. Eventually turned life around.
Great-Grandfather's Surname	Buckner	
Great-Great Grandfather's Surname	Could not trace	
Great-Great-Great Grandfather's Surname	Could not trace	
Great Grandfather's (4x) Surname	Could not trace	

Note: Tracing your family's lineage and choices may require you to have some uncomfortable conversations with distant or estranged family members. Prioritize your deliverance over your discomfort.

PATERNAL

Trace your father's surname up to seven generations. Note: you should share or have shared (for married women) the same surname as your father, but if your parents were unmarried, the generational curse of dishonor may have started through them or they may have been repeating it. Trace fornication, adultery and every other issue of dishonor and renounce it. If at all possible, interview the older people in your family and ask as many questions as possible.

Generations	Surnames	Generational Issue/ Event
Your Surname		
Father's Surname		
Grandfather's Surname		
Great-Grandfather's Surname		
Great-Great Grandfather's Surname		
Great-Great-Great Grandfather's Surname		
Great Grandfather's (4x) Surname		

Paternal (Notes)

MATERNAL

Trace your mother's surname up to seven generations. Trace fornication, adultery and every other issue of dishonor and renounce it. If at all possible, interview the older people in your family and ask as many questions as possible.

Generations	Surnames	Generational Issue/ Event
Your Surname		
Father's Surname		
Grandfather's Surname		
Great-Grandfather's Surname		
Great-Great Grandfather's Surname		
Great-Great-Great Grandfather's Surname		
Great Grandfather's (4x) Surname		

Maternal (Notes)

How to Use This Manual

This is a yearly devotional and journal. The goal of this guide is to help you trace your issues, track your success and train or discipline your flesh until you reach your highest potential. Esther was prepared for her king for 12 months, but she had been prepared for the King of kings her entire life. This guide is designed to serve as a measuring stick of your deliverance and maturity.

This guide is divided up into twelve parts, starting at Month One and ending at Month Twelve. Each month, you'll find the following:
- Crown Jewel: The Crown Jewel is wisdom designed to transform your mind, your perspective and, of course, your life.
- Love Letter from Heaven: This is a short, but encouraging letter to you written to help you better understand who you are and why you're here.
- The Story of Esther: The book of Esther has ten chapters, and for the first ten chapters of this guide, you will find one of those books. The remaining two chapters are also headed up by a scripture. Read each chapter, stopping to highlight the words that jump out at you. This will help you to better understand the story and empathize with Esther's plight. After that, use the provided boxes to detail what you've learned from each chapter. *See example below.* (Note: Please do the exercise below to start. The words have already been highlighted for you in this exercise.)

> You'll notice that I highlighted certain words in the verses of scripture (*below*). The goal of this is to open your eyes and your mind to the heart of the Author, and not just to the text. After reading each verse, you'll notice that your understanding is not only opened, but that the text suddenly has come to life.
>
> In every chapter, you will come across scriptures, but they will not be highlighted. To get the most out of the text, be sure to highlight the words that stand out to you before answering the questions.

Queens & Things

```
Y L V I C T O R Y V R N X A R
K O L Y I G C A S T L E E N O
P R I N C E S S M L T J R O Y
Q D M B W P R I N C E E X I A
D E L I V E R A N C E W E N L
Z L A V I S H L O V E S S T T
Y H S N R L E G A L I T Y E Y
O Y O T H R O N E K I N G D Y
Q Z K N A C D I G N I F I E D
V U Y I O F O Q H K N R E X O
A N E F N R F U E Z T E S J C
S O V E G G A F R B I G T E R
H B P I N K D B O T A A H S O
T L G L V W G O L O R L E U W
I E P R E T T Y M E A P R S N
```

Deliverance	Dignified	Honorable	Legality
Victory	Kingdom	Royalty	Anointed
Throne	Xerxes	Pretty	Esther
Castle	Tiara	Prince	Court
Queen	Staff	Regal	Lavish
Princess	Vashti	Crown	Jesus
Noble	Jews	Pink	Love
Lord	Hero	King	

Answer key at back of book

Proverbs 31	Verse
10	Who can find a virtuous woman? For her price is far above rubies
11	The heart of her husband doth safely trust in her, so that he shall have no need of spoil.
12	She will do him good and not evil all the days of her life.
13	She seeketh wool, and flax, and worketh willingly with her hands.
14	She is like the merchants' ships; she bringeth her food from afar.
15	She riseth also while it is yet night, and giveth meat to her household, and a portion to her maidens.
16	She considereth a field, and buyeth it: with the fruit of her hands she planteth a vineyard.
17	She girdeth her loins with strength, and strengtheneth her arms.
18	She perceiveth that her merchandise is good: her candle goeth not out by night.
19	She layeth her hands to the spindle, and her hands hold the distaff.
20	She stretcheth out her hand to the poor; yea, she reacheth forth her hands to the needy.
21	She is not afraid of the snow for her household: for all her household are clothed with scarlet.
22	She maketh herself coverings of tapestry; her clothing is silk and purple.
23	Her husband is known in the gates, when he sitteth among the elders of the land.
24	She maketh fine linen, and selleth it; and delivereth girdles unto the merchant.
25	Strength and honour are her clothing; and she shall rejoice in time to come.
26	She openeth her mouth with wisdom; and in her tongue is the law of kindness.
27	She looketh well to the ways of her household, and eateth not the bread of idleness.

28	Her children arise up, and call her blessed; her husband also, and he praiseth her.
29	Many daughters have done virtuously, but thou excellest them all.
30	Favor is deceitful, and beauty is vain: but a woman that feareth the LORD, she shall be praised.
31	Give her of the fruit of her hands; and let her own works praise her in the gates.

Notes

Notes

Notes

Proverbs 31	What Revelation Did You Extract from Each Verse?
10	
11	
12	
13	
14	
15	
16	
17	

18

19

20

21

22

23

24

25

26

27	
28	
29	
30	
31	

Every month, you will also find the following:
- Esther Tracer: Use this tool to trace and track your fears and other issues. Please note that they should be less and less every month. If your list of issues remain the same or continues to grow from month to month, you may need to seek out deliverance and counseling. Also, using the Esther Tracer, list what you're doing to combat each issue. For example, if you deal with rejection, what books on rejection are you reading, what seminars have you attended and what methods are you imploring to free yourself from this bondage?
- Esther's Trail: In this section, you will find a list of events and challenges to take. The goal is for you to monitor your movement. This keeps you from being stagnant and

immobile. In this section, you will place the date besides every event or activity you participate in.

- Prayer Closet: This section lists a prayer for you to pray each month.
- Challenge of the Month: Here, you will find a set of instructions or challenges to take each month. Don't skip a month! These challenges are designed to stretch and pull you outside of your comfort zone.
- Esther's Edict: Every month, you will find an edict to declare over yourself. An edict is a legal decree set in place by someone in authority.
- Esther Tracker: Here, you will journal about the challenges you face each month, and what you've done to facilitate your growth and maturity.

You will also find:

- Personal Constitution (back of book): This is a tool designed to help you establish a system of self-governance which, in turn, will help you better develop self-control and all of the fruits needed to be a healthy, whole and prosperous individual.

Month One

From Hardship to Leadership

CROWN JEWEL I

Esther was no stranger to tragedy. She'd been orphaned as a child, and while the Bible does not tell us how her parents died, what we do know is that her cousin, Mordecai, took her in and raised her as his own. Like many women, Esther cried many nights, wondering why every other woman around her had a "normal" life, while her life was anything but normal. She may have been ostracized, rejected and laughed at by her peers simply because her life didn't look like theirs. And while there is no evidence of this, if we look at humankind from the beginning of time, we will see a trend that has been consistent throughout history. That trend is—people tend to cast away, bully, make fun of, reject and even attack people who are (in their minds) "less than" themselves or, at minimum, different than the personality types they are accustomed to. This is largely because humans tend to be intimidated by people who stand out. Even when you stand out because of tragedy, you are still standing out; this catapults you into the spotlight, causing people who operate as the alpha males or females of a community, program, school, organization, family, etc. to take notice of you. In their attempt to reinforce their positions and power, they may mishandle, attack or humiliate you. In other words, tragedy may have tossed you into the spotlight, but that's because God was fitting you for your crown.

HEAVEN'S LOVE LETTER TO YOU

Dear Queen,
Sometimes, some of the greatest leaders didn't chase spotlights or platforms, they were tossed into the spotlight by tragedy. In other words, they were "accidental" leaders before they accepted their roles in purpose on purpose.

Life may have been harder for you than most women, but this may be because God was getting you ready for the crown you're set to wear. Don't look at your story as a tragic one. See it as a unique story that's being written for others to see what the journey looks like from the pit to the palace.

Esther 1

Now in the days of Ahasuerus, the Ahasuerus who reigned from India to Ethiopia over 127 provinces, in those days when King Ahasuerus sat on his royal throne in Susa, the citadel, in the third year of his reign he gave a feast for all his officials and servants. The army of Persia and Media and the nobles and governors of the provinces were before him, while he showed the riches of his royal glory and the splendor and pomp of his greatness for many days, 180 days. And when these days were completed, the king gave for all the people present in Susa the citadel, both great and small, a feast lasting for seven days in the court of the garden of the king's palace. There were white cotton curtains and violet hangings fastened with cords of fine linen and purple to silver rods and marble pillars, and also couches of gold and silver on a mosaic pavement of porphyry, marble, mother-of-pearl, and precious stones. Drinks were served in golden vessels, vessels of different kinds, and the royal wine was lavished according to the bounty of the king. And drinking was according to this edict: "There is no compulsion." For the king had given orders to all the staff of his palace to do as each man desired. Queen Vashti also gave a feast for the women in the palace that belonged to King Ahasuerus.

On the seventh day, when the heart of the king was merry with wine, he commanded Mehuman, Biztha, Harbona, Bigtha and Abagtha, Zethar and Carkas, the seven eunuchs who served in the presence of King Ahasuerus, to bring Queen Vashti before the king with her royal crown, in order to show the peoples and the princes her beauty, for she was lovely to look at. But Queen Vashti refused to come at the king's command delivered by the eunuchs. At this the king became enraged, and his anger burned within him.

Then the king said to the wise men who knew the times (for this was the king's procedure toward all who were versed in law and judgment, the men next to him being Carshena, Shethar, Admatha, Tarshish, Meres, Marsena, and Memucan, the seven princes of Persia and Media, who saw the king's face, and sat first in the kingdom): "According to the law, what is to be done to Queen Vashti, because she has not performed the command of King Ahasuerus delivered by the eunuchs?" Then Memucan said in the presence of the king and the officials, "Not only against the king has Queen Vashti done wrong, but also against all the officials and all the peoples who are in all the provinces of King Ahasuerus. For the queen's behavior will be made known to all women, causing them to look at their husbands with contempt, since they will say, 'King Ahasuerus commanded Queen Vashti to be brought before him, and she did not come.' This very day the noble women of Persia and Media who have heard of the queen's behavior will say the same to all the king's officials, and there will be contempt and wrath in plenty. If it please the king, let a royal order go out from him, and let it be written among the laws of the Persians and the Medes so that it may not be repealed, that Vashti is never again to come before King Ahasuerus. And let the king give her royal position to another who is better than she. So when the decree made by the king is proclaimed throughout all his kingdom, for it is vast, all women will give honor to their husbands, high and low alike." This advice pleased the king and the princes, and the king did as Memucan proposed. He sent letters to all the royal provinces, to every province in its own script and to every people in its own language, that every man be master in his own household and speak according to the language of his people.

WHAT HAVE YOU LEARNED FROM THE SCRIPTURE AND VERSES ABOVE, AND HOW DO YOU PLAN TO APPLY WHAT YOU'VE LEARNED TO YOUR LIFE?

1	
2	
3	
4	
5	
6	
7	

8	
9	
10	
11	
12	
13	
14	
15	

Esther Tracer

(Month One)

List your fears and other issues, trace them all the way to their roots, and then list what you're going to do to train them. How do you plan to get free? What books are you reading? Who's your therapist? What programs are you in? If you want to grow, heal and be delivered, you have to be intentional and consistent with monitoring and managing your mind.

List Each Fear/ Insecurity/ Issue	Trace Each Fear and Insecurity	Train Each Fear and Insecurity

Esther's Trail

(Month One)

Any time you participate in any of the events listed below, be sure to pencil in the date. Note, you can write as many dates into one window that you can fit into each space. The goal is to teach you to enjoy your own company.

Event	Dates	Event	Dates
Did Something Nice for Myself		Went to Church	
Dined in Restaurant		Studied Bible	
Exercised		Went to Church	
Encouraged Someone		Studied Bible	
Blessed Someone		Went to Church	
Overcame an Offense		Studied Bible	
Expressed Myself Creatively		Went to Church	
Resisted Temptation		Studied Bible	
Learned Something New		Went to Church	
Broke Cultural Barriers		Studied Bible	
Challenged Myself		Went to Church	

PRAYER CLOSET

Esther's Prayer

Dear Lord,

I come before You asking You to heal me of all of my traumas, hurts and rejection. I commit my heart, mind and soul to You. I am the clay, You are the Potter. I ask that You mold me into the woman You designed me to be. Help me to forgive everyone who has trespassed against me and help me to forgive myself. If I'm angry or upset with You for any reason, help me to forgive You. I realize more than anything that I need You in every way. I love and honor You, and I submit myself to You with all of my might.

It is in Jesus name that I pray,

Amen.

CHALLENGE OF THE MONTH

Esther's Deliverance

List all of your past traumas and renounce them. You can say, for example, I renounce the rejection that came in when my father abandoned me. I choose to forgive him and I command the pain, the fear, and the insecurities that came in through that rejection to leave me now—in Jesus name!

ESTHER'S EDICT

Esther's Confession

I am beautifully and wonderfully made! I am the righteousness of God in Christ Jesus! No weapon that is formed against me or my family will prosper, and every tongue that rises against us in judgment, God has already condemned. I am not what happened to me. I am royalty. I am created in the image and likeness of God. I am whole. I am healed. I am free.

ESTHER TRACKER

(Month One)

This is your journal for the month. List upcoming events, past incidents, your fears, your concerns, your expectations, your hopes, how you intend to respond to the issues you're facing, how you've responded to each issue/incident that you have faced (this month), and how you plan to improve so that you'll be a better woman next month.

If you need more space to write, please use a notebook, but be sure to get it all out.

Before you move on to the journal, please write a note/declaration to yourself (in the box below), detailing how you intend to manage this month.

NOTE TO SELF

Week One

Week Two

Week Three

Week Four

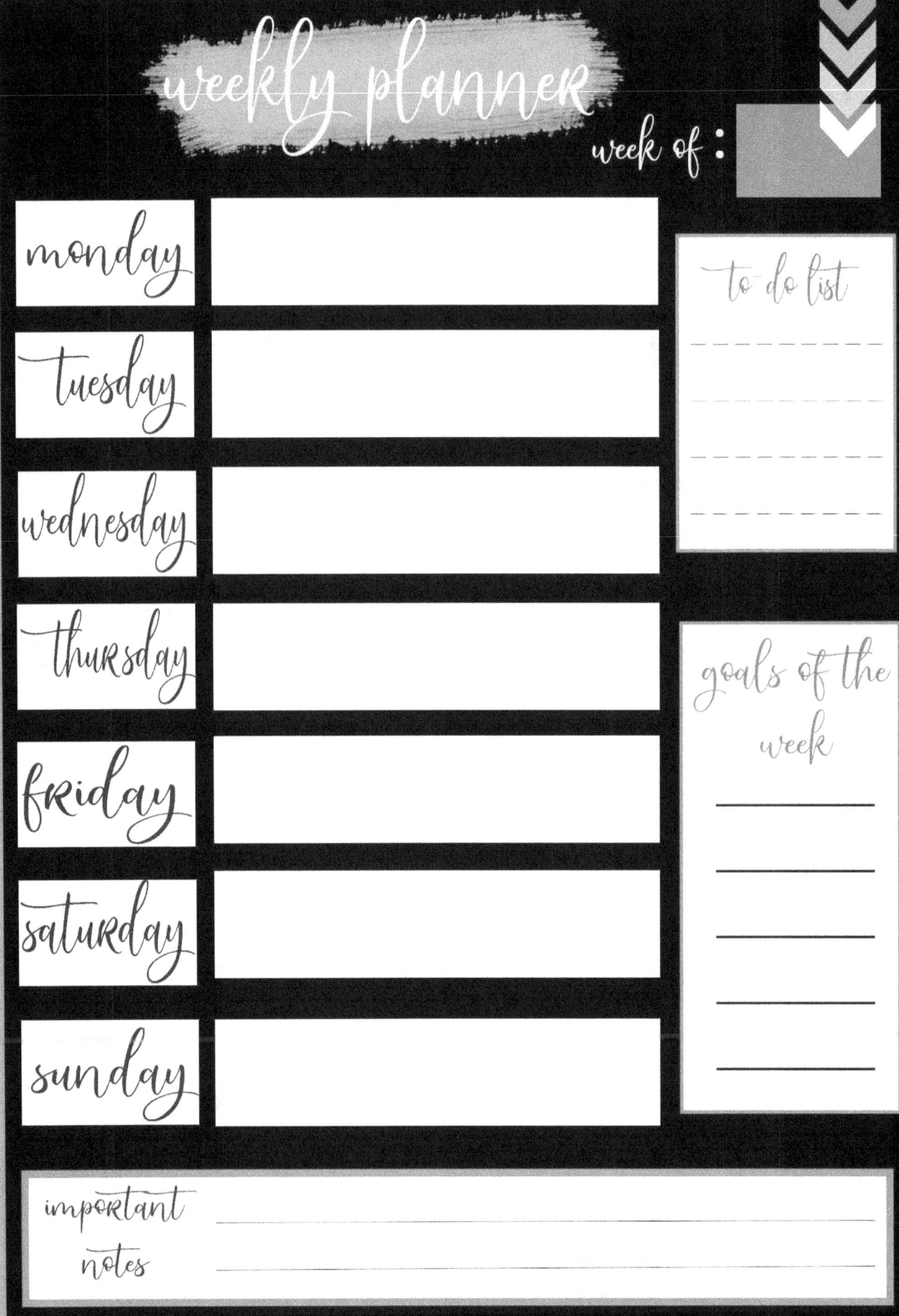

Month Two

BREAK THE CURSE

CROWN JEWEL II

Did you know that the word "maiden" means "virgin"? What this means is that your maiden name is your "virgin name." It is the name of your father (or someone's father), and it was passed down to you so that you could honor his legacy; that is, until a man comes along and attaches his surname to you. Having sex with a woman outside of marriage, both traditionally and non-traditionally, are considered to be crimes against the woman's father. This is called a crime of dishonor. Why? Because it leaves a stain on the father's name. In the Biblical era, such a crime could cause the Hebrew community to judge the father of the young woman as immoral, untrustworthy and ungodly. Consequently, no one would want to trade with him, marry any of his daughters or allow his sons to marry their daughters. This bad reputation would attach itself to the father's name—a name that would be shared with his sons, and it would follow that family generation after generation. This is the very picture of a generational curse!

If you look at biblical history, you'll notice that all generational curses started with dishonor. What this tells us is that God's system of honor must be established and followed through, otherwise, sin would sweep through and pervert the land.

HEAVEN'S LOVE LETTER TO YOU

Dear Queen,

Like many queens before you, you may not be a virgin. You've made mistakes in your quest to love and to be loved. And like most queens, you've probably never experienced true, authentic, pure love (with no motives attached), so you don't necessarily know what to look for. This is why God said in Matthew 6:33, "But seek first the kingdom of God and his righteousness, and all these things will be added to you." According to the Word, God is Love. In other words, Love is not a feeling, Love is a person. And until you discover the person of Love, you'll keep settling for dopamine-driven relationships that fail as soon as one or both parties involved sober up. This is your opportunity to take the shattered pieces of your soul back, and let God put you back together again so that the right man and/or the right opportunities will find you; this is your opportunity to break the generational curse of divorce, fatherlessness and every other issue that has plagued your bloodline. But first, you have to seek and find the Lord; this way, He can help you to discover yourself.

You can do it. You were built for this! Will it be easy? No! But is it worth it? Absolutely! And remember, Love breaks the curse!

Esther 2

After these things, when the anger of King Ahasuerus had abated, he remembered Vashti and what she had done and what had been decreed against her. Then the king's young men who attended him said, "Let beautiful young virgins be sought out for the king. And let the king appoint officers in all the provinces of his kingdom to gather all the beautiful young virgins to the harem in Susa the citadel, under custody of Hegai, the king's eunuch, who is in charge of the women. Let their cosmetics be given them. And let the young woman who pleases the king be queen instead of Vashti." This pleased the king, and he did so.

Now there was a Jew in Susa the citadel whose name was Mordecai, the son of Jair, son of Shimei, son of Kish, a Benjaminite, who had been carried away from Jerusalem among the captives carried away with Jeconiah king of Judah, whom Nebuchadnezzar king of Babylon had carried away. He was bringing up Hadassah, that is Esther, the daughter of his uncle, for she had neither father nor mother. The young woman had a beautiful figure and was lovely to look at, and when her father and her mother died, Mordecai took her as his own daughter. So when the king's order and his edict were proclaimed, and when many young women were gathered in Susa the citadel in custody of Hegai, Esther also was taken into the king's palace and put in custody of Hegai, who had charge of the women. And the young woman pleased him and won his favor. And he quickly provided her with her cosmetics and her portion of food, and with seven chosen young women from the king's palace, and advanced her and her young women to the best place in the harem. Esther had not made known her people or kindred, for Mordecai had commanded her not to make it known. And every day Mordecai walked in front of the court of the harem to learn how Esther was and what was happening to her.

Now when the turn came for each young woman to go in to King Ahasuerus, after being twelve months under the regulations for the women, since this was the regular period of their beautifying, six months with oil of myrrh and six months with spices and ointments for women — when the young woman went in to the king in this way, she was given whatever she desired to take with her from the harem to the king's palace. In the evening she would go in, and in the morning she would return to the second harem in custody of Shaashgaz, the king's eunuch, who was in charge of the concubines. She would not go in to the king again, unless the king delighted in her and she was summoned by name.

When the turn came for Esther the daughter of Abihail the uncle of Mordecai, who had taken her as his own daughter, to go in to the king, she asked for nothing except what Hegai the king's eunuch, who had charge of the women, advised. Now Esther was winning favor in the eyes of all who saw her. And when Esther was taken to King Ahasuerus, into his royal palace, in the tenth month, which is the month of Tebeth, in the seventh year of his reign, the king loved Esther more than all the women, and she won grace and favor in his sight more than all the virgins, so that he set the royal crown on her head and made her queen instead of Vashti. Then the king gave a great feast for all his officials and servants; it was Esther's feast. He also granted a remission of taxes to the provinces and gave gifts with royal generosity.

Now when the virgins were gathered together the second time, Mordecai was sitting at the king's gate. Esther had not made known her kindred or her people, as Mordecai had commanded her, for Esther obeyed Mordecai just as when she was brought up by him. In those days, as Mordecai was sitting at the king's gate, Bigthan and Teresh, two of the king's eunuchs, who guarded the threshold, became angry and sought to lay hands on King Ahasuerus. And this came to the knowledge of Mordecai, and he told it to Queen Esther, and Esther told the king in the name of Mordecai. When the affair was investigated and found to be so, the men were both hanged on the gallows. And it was recorded in the book of the chronicles in the presence of the king.

WHAT HAVE YOU LEARNED FROM THE SCRIPTURE AND VERSES ABOVE, AND HOW DO YOU PLAN TO APPLY WHAT YOU'VE LEARNED TO YOUR LIFE?

1

2

3

4

5

6	
7	
8	
9	
10	
11	
12	
13	
14	

ESTHER TRACER
(Month Two)

List your fears and other issues, trace them all the way to their roots, and then list what you're going to do to train them. How do you plan to get free? What books are you reading? Who's your therapist? What programs are you in? If you want to grow, heal and be delivered, you have to be intentional and consistent with monitoring and managing your mind.

List Each Fear/ Insecurity/ Issue	Trace Each Fear and Insecurity	Train Each Fear and Insecurity

ESTHER'S TRAIL

(Month Two)

Any time you participate in any of the events listed below, be sure to pencil in the date. Note, you can write as many dates into one window that you can fit into each space. The goal is to teach you to enjoy your own company.

Event	Dates	Event	Dates
Did Something Nice for Myself		Went to Church	
Dined in Restaurant		Studied Bible	
Exercised		Went to Church	
Encouraged Someone		Studied Bible	
Blessed Someone		Went to Church	
Overcame an Offense		Studied Bible	
Expressed Myself Creatively		Went to Church	
Resisted Temptation		Studied Bible	
Learned Something New		Went to Church	
Broke Cultural Barriers		Studied Bible	
Challenged Myself		Went to Church	

PRAYER CLOSET

Esther's Prayer

Dear Lord,
Thank You for Your unfailing love and grace. I ask that You restore to me all the years that the locusts have eaten, and all that the cankerworm, the caterpillar and the palmerworm have devoured. Restore my trust in You, restore my heart (make me whole again) and restore my peace. Don't let me quit on myself, and more than anything, don't let me quit on You. I ask that You keep and guide me, and when the storms start raging up against me, I ask that You send Your ministering angels to encourage me and fight on my behalf. I give You all the praise, honor and the glory for who You are and all You've done.
It is in Jesus name that I pray,
Amen.

CHALLENGE OF THE MONTH

Esther's Deliverance

List all of the generational curses in your family that you can find. Trace them by interviewing some of the older people in your family. Keep records. Use the audio feature on your phone to record their responses. Be sure to let them know you're recording what they say. Repent and renounce those strongholds and ask the Lord to set you free from them.

ESTHER'S EDICT

Esther's Confession

I am not my mother. I am not my father. I am a new person and this is a new day. The curses end with me. I will be a blessing to everyone that I know and everywhere that I go. Peace is my inheritance. Joy is my inheritance. I am blessed going out and blessed coming in. I am a new day.

ESTHER TRACKER

(Month Two)

This is your journal for the month. List upcoming events, past incidents, your fears, your concerns, your expectations, your hopes, how you intend to respond to the issues you're facing, how you've responded to each issue/incident that you have faced (this month), and how you plan to improve so that you'll be a better woman next month.

If you need more space to write, please use a notebook, but be sure to get it all out.

Before you move on to the journal, please write a note/declaration to yourself (in the box below), detailing how you intend to manage this month.

Note to Self

Week One

Week Two

Week Three

Week Four

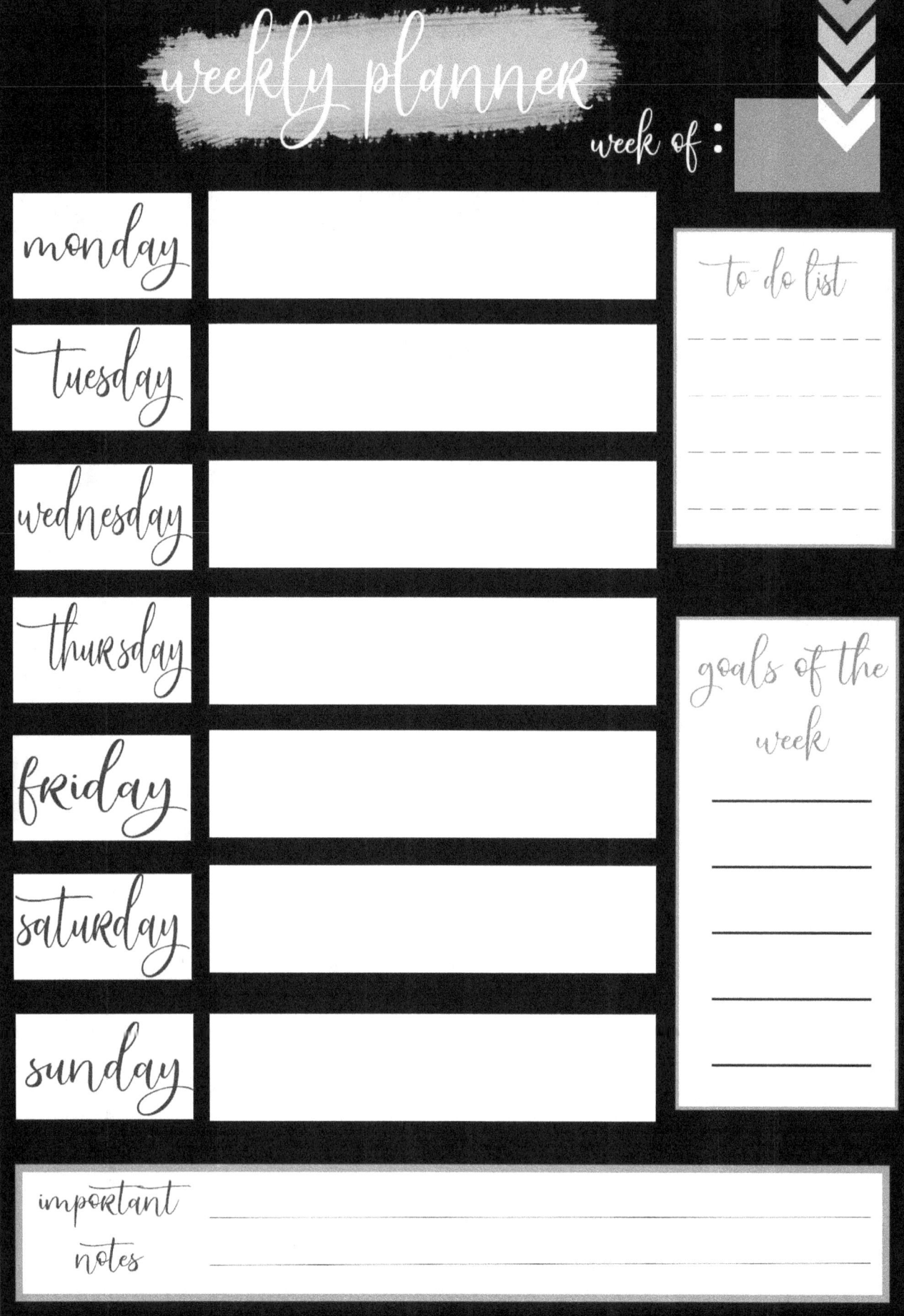

Month Three

FITTING INTO YOUR CROWN

CROWN JEWEL III

Galatians 4:1-5 reads, "Now I say, That the heir, as long as he is a child, differeth nothing from a servant, though he be lord of all; but is under tutors and governors until the time appointed of the father. Even so we, when we were children, were in bondage under the elements of the world: But when the fullness of the time was come, God sent forth his Son, made of a woman, made under the law, to redeem them that were under the law, that we might receive the adoption of sons."

Another word for "servant" is "slave." What this scripture is telling us is this—a man or woman set to inherit a fortune (tangible wealth or wisdom) must mature before he or she is eligible to tap into that wealth. And when the scripture uses the word "child," the author is not referencing the age of an individual, but more so the maturity of an individual.

Your maturity is seen in your response to the many events of life, especially negative stimuli. An immature response is an emotional one, but a mature response is a logical one, especially one provoked by love.

HEAVEN'S LOVE LETTER TO YOU

Dear Queen,

There may be some blessings hovering over your bloodline that have not yet landed because no one in your family has broken the generational curses that have plagued your family for hundreds, if not thousands of years. Remember this—God's promises to you are "yes" and "amen," but the manifestations of those promises are waiting for you to grow up.

Growing up or, better yet, maturing isn't incidental, it's an intentional act. In other words, you have to address your issues, repent (turn away from your sins) and learn how to love, live and think as a queen. Understand this—when God said, "He who finds a wife finds a good thing and obtains favor of the Lord," He wasn't referencing a man marrying a woman. When He uses the term "wife," He's talking about a mindset; He's talking about a mature, God-fearing woman who knows (and respects) who she is. This means that in order to be found, you must first be hidden and developed. You need leaders and mentors to help you to break through toxic thinking patterns and habits that disqualify you for your earthly inheritance.

Queen, don't be in a rush to make yourself seen. Don't rush God's promises. He hides you while He develops you, but in order to stay hidden, you must respect your hiding place as well as the process. Don't let jealousy, competition, comparison, rejection, abandonment or hurt cause you to abort the process!

Esther 3

After these things King Ahasuerus promoted Haman the Agagite, the son of Hammedatha, and advanced him and set his throne above all the officials who were with him. And all the king's servants who were at the king's gate bowed down and paid homage to Haman, for the king had so commanded concerning him. But Mordecai did not bow down or pay homage. Then the king's servants who were at the king's gate said to Mordecai, "Why do you transgress the king's command?" And when they spoke to him day after day and he would not listen to them, they told Haman, in order to see whether Mordecai's words would stand, for he had told them that he was a Jew. And when Haman saw that Mordecai did not bow down or pay homage to him, Haman was filled with fury. But he disdained to lay hands on Mordecai alone. So, as they had made known to him the people of Mordecai, Haman sought to destroy all the Jews, the people of Mordecai, throughout the whole kingdom of Ahasuerus.

In the first month, which is the month of Nisan, in the twelfth year of King Ahasuerus, they cast Pur (that is, they cast lots) before Haman day after day; and they cast it month after month till the twelfth month, which is the month of Adar. Then Haman said to King Ahasuerus, "There is a certain people scattered abroad and dispersed among the peoples in all the provinces of your kingdom. Their laws are different from those of every other people, and they do not keep the king's laws, so that it is not to the king's profit to tolerate them. If it please the king, let it be decreed that they be destroyed, and I will pay 10,000 talents of silver into the hands of those who have charge of the king's business, that they may put it into the king's treasuries." So the king took his signet ring from his hand and gave it to Haman the Agagite, the son of Hammedatha, the enemy of the Jews. And the king said to Haman, "The money is given to you, the people also, to do with them as it seems good to you."

Then the king's scribes were summoned on the thirteenth day of the first month, and an edict, according to all that Haman commanded, was written to the king's satraps and to the governors over all the provinces and to the officials of all the peoples, to every province in its own script and every people in its own language. It was written in the name of King Ahasuerus and sealed with the king's signet ring. Letters were sent by couriers to all the king's provinces with instruction to destroy, to kill, and to annihilate all Jews, young and old, women and children, in one day, the thirteenth day of the twelfth month, which is the month of Adar, and to plunder their goods. A copy of the document was to be issued as a decree in every province by proclamation to all the peoples to be ready for that day. The couriers went out hurriedly by order of the king, and the decree was issued in Susa the citadel. And the king and Haman sat down to drink, but the city of Susa was thrown into confusion.

What have you learned from the scripture and verses above, and how do you plan to apply what you've learned to your life?

1.

2.

3.

4.

5.

6.

7.

8.

9	
10	
11	
12	
13	
14	
15	

ESTHER TRACER
(Month Three)

List your fears and other issues, trace them all the way to their roots, and then list what you're going to do to train them. How do you plan to get free? What books are you reading? Who's your therapist? What programs are you in? If you want to grow, heal and be delivered, you have to be intentional and consistent with monitoring and managing your mind.

List Each Fear/ Insecurity/ Issue	Trace Each Fear and Insecurity	Train Each Fear and Insecurity

ESTHER'S TRAIL

(Month Three)

Any time you participate in any of the events listed below, be sure to pencil in the date. Note, you can write as many dates into one window that you can fit into each space. The goal is to teach you to enjoy your own company.

Event	Dates	Event	Dates
Did Something Nice for Myself		Went to Church	
Dined in Restaurant		Studied Bible	
Exercised		Went to Church	
Encouraged Someone		Studied Bible	
Blessed Someone		Went to Church	
Overcame an Offense		Studied Bible	
Expressed Myself Creatively		Went to Church	
Resisted Temptation		Studied Bible	
Learned Something New		Went to Church	
Broke Cultural Barriers		Studied Bible	
Challenged Myself		Went to Church	

PRAYER CLOSET

Esther's Prayer

Dear Lord,
You are good, You are faithful and You are merciful. Hide me until You're ready to reveal me. Heal me as You grow me up in you. Whatever blessings that have been hovering over my family, I ask that You prepare my heart and my mind to receive them. Lord, please save and heal my family members as well. Let Your name be glorified in all that I do and say.
It is in Jesus name that I pray,
Amen.

CHALLENGE OF THE MONTH

Esther's Deliverance

List all of the generational blessings and gifts in your family that you can sense, but not necessarily trace. For example, you may notice that most of the women in your family can sing relatively well. Ask the Lord to restore your gifts and rebuke any and every unclean spirit that may be assigned to hinder, attack, pervert and limit those gifts.

ESTHER'S EDICT

Esther's Confession

I am a gift. I am a masterpiece because I was created by the Master. I am healed. I am favored. I am my authentic self. Generational blessings are my portion. I will start many of the generational blessings that my descendants will someday enjoy. Everything that I touch is blessed. Favor follows me. The blessings of the Lord make me rich, and He adds no sorrow to them.

ESTHER TRACKER
(Month Three)

This is your journal for the month. List upcoming events, past incidents, your fears, your concerns, your expectations, your hopes, how you intend to respond to the issues you're facing, how you've responded to each issue/incident that you have faced (this month), and how you plan to improve so that you'll be a better woman next month.

If you need more space to write, please use a notebook, but be sure to get it all out.

Before you move on to the journal, please write a note/declaration to yourself (in the box below), detailing how you intend to manage this month.

NOTE TO SELF

Week One

Week Two

Week Three

Week Four

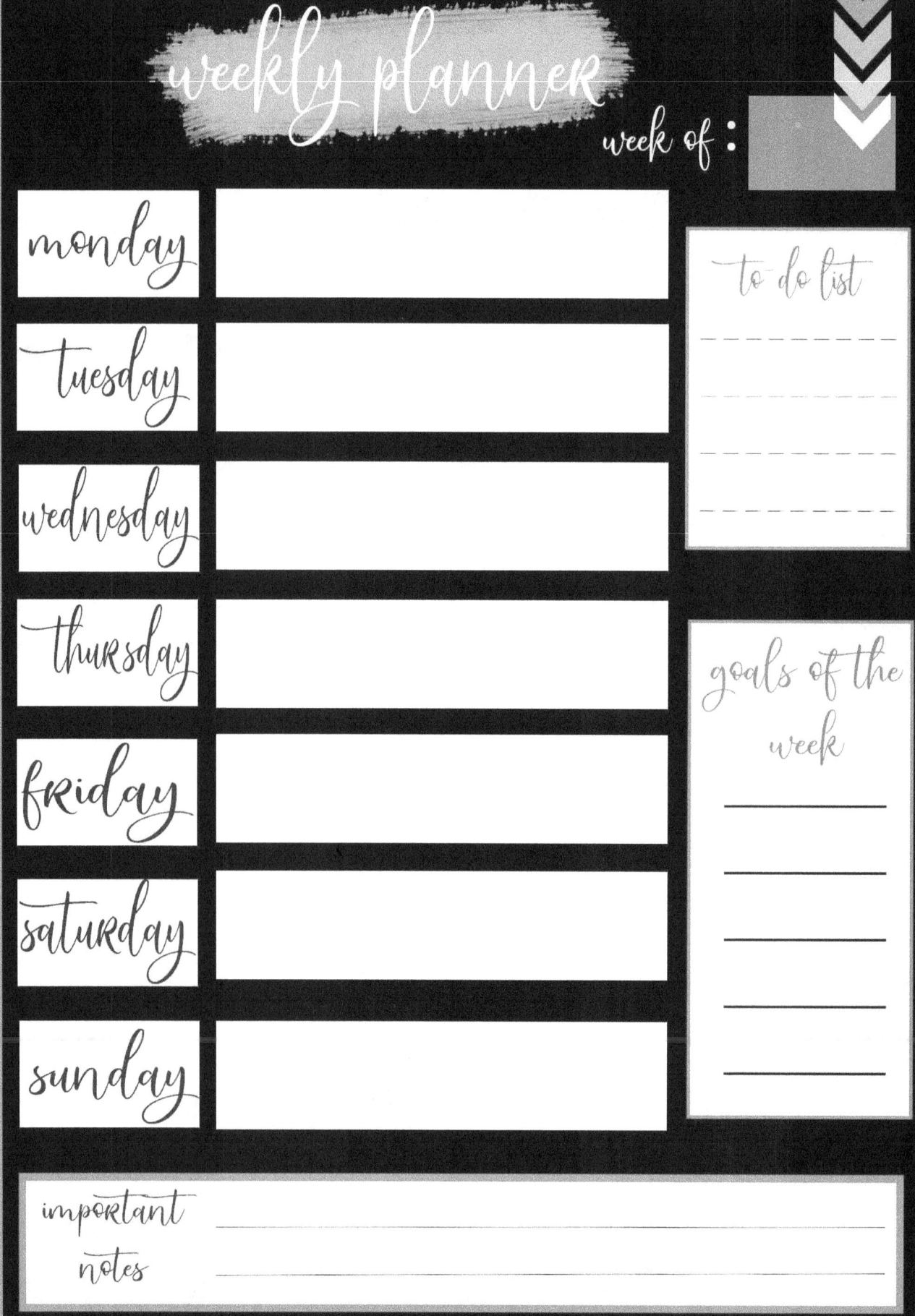

Month Four

THE POWER OF SUBMISSION

CROWN JEWEL IV

A problem arose in paradise. That problem's name was Haman. And while Haman appeared to be a giant of a problem, God had already developed a David-like solution named Esther, but her weapon of choice would not be a rock and a sling. it would be one of the most powerful, but disregarded weapons that a woman can ever possess, and that is submission.

Submission. Most women today are absolutely terrified of this word because they automatically think about the men who've abused and mishandled them. How could someone in their right mind tell them to submit to those men? This is because they don't realize that there are men out there who can be trusted to lead them, but they have to be pruned, developed, matured and hidden before they can be found by men of this stature. Esther submitted to Mordecai. This is where she got the training she would need to submit to the king. And it was her beauty that got her in the castle, her humility that caused the king to place the crown on her head, but it was her submission that saved an entire nation of people.

Heaven's Love Letter to You

Dear Queen,
When (or if) your father rejected or mishandled you, Satan was attacking your submission. When that ex of yours promised to love you all the days of your life, he was a weapon formed against your submission. You see, Satan knew that if he could keep you from being a submissive wife, he could get you to relinquish your rightful position to take a lower one. The word "submit" is not a cursed word, it's a weapon, and a powerful one at that! Surround yourself with women who gracefully demonstrate the art of submission and you will see that it's nothing to fear. Of course, submission is not to be confused with fear and passivity. A woman who truly submits does so because she trusts the authorities in her life to lead her or, better yet, she trusts God to lead her through the people He's placed in authority in her life.

Esther 4

When Mordecai learned all that had been done, Mordecai tore his clothes and put on sackcloth and ashes, and went out into the midst of the city, and he cried out with a loud and bitter cry. He went up to the entrance of the king's gate, for no one was allowed to enter the king's gate clothed in sackcloth. And in every province, wherever the king's command and his decree reached, there was great mourning among the Jews, with fasting and weeping and lamenting, and many of them lay in sackcloth and ashes.

When Esther's young women and her eunuchs came and told her, the queen was deeply distressed. She sent garments to clothe Mordecai, so that he might take off his sackcloth, but he would not accept them. Then Esther called for Hathach, one of the king's eunuchs, who had been appointed to attend her, and ordered him to go to Mordecai to learn what this was and why it was. Hathach went out to Mordecai in the open square of the city in front of the king's gate, and Mordecai told him all that had happened to him, and the exact sum of money that Haman had promised to pay into the king's treasuries for the destruction of the Jews. Mordecai also gave him a copy of the written decree issued in Susa for their destruction, that he might show it to Esther and explain it to her and command her to go to the king to beg his favor and plead with him on behalf of her people. And Hathach went and told Esther what Mordecai had said. Then Esther spoke to Hathach and commanded him to go to Mordecai and say, "All the king's servants and the people of the king's provinces know that if any man or woman goes to the king inside the inner court without being called, there is but one law—to be put to death, except the one to whom the king holds out the golden scepter so that he may live. But as for me, I have not been called to come in to the king these thirty days."

And they told Mordecai what Esther had said. Then Mordecai told them to reply to Esther, "Do not think to yourself that in the king's palace you will escape any more than all the other Jews. For if you keep silent at this time, relief and deliverance will rise for the Jews from another place, but you and your father's house will perish. And who knows whether you have not come to the kingdom for such a time as this?" Then Esther told them to reply to Mordecai, "Go, gather all the Jews to be found in Susa, and hold a fast on my behalf, and do not eat or drink for three days, night or day. I and my young women will also fast as you do. Then I will go to the king, though it is against the law, and if I perish, I perish." Mordecai then went away and did everything as Esther had ordered him.

WHAT HAVE YOU LEARNED FROM THE SCRIPTURE AND VERSES ABOVE, AND HOW DO YOU PLAN TO APPLY WHAT YOU'VE LEARNED TO YOUR LIFE?

1.

2.

3.

4.

5.

6.

7.

8.

| 9 |
| 10 |
| 11 |
| 12 |
| 13 |
| 14 |
| 15 |

ESTHER TRACER
(Month Four)

List your fears and other issues, trace them all the way to their roots, and then list what you're going to do to train them. How do you plan to get free? What books are you reading? Who's your therapist? What programs are you in? If you want to grow, heal and be delivered, you have to be intentional and consistent with monitoring and managing your mind.

List Each Fear/ Insecurity/ Issue	Trace Each Fear and Insecurity	Train Each Fear and Insecurity

Esther's Trail

(Month Four)

Any time you participate in any of the events listed below, be sure to pencil in the date. Note, you can write as many dates into one window that you can fit into each space. The goal is to teach you to enjoy your own company.

Event	Dates	Event	Dates
Did Something Nice for Myself		Went to Church	
Dined in Restaurant		Studied Bible	
Exercised		Went to Church	
Encouraged Someone		Studied Bible	
Blessed Someone		Went to Church	
Overcame an Offense		Studied Bible	
Expressed Myself Creatively		Went to Church	
Resisted Temptation		Studied Bible	
Learned Something New		Went to Church	
Broke Cultural Barriers		Studied Bible	
Challenged Myself		Went to Church	

PRAYER CLOSET

Esther's Prayer

Dear Lord,
Teach me more about honor. Remove the scales from my eyes so that I can see honor, submission and love in their purest forms. Take away my fear of submission and deliver me from the fear of authority or authority figures. Send people for me to submit to, and give me the grace, the humility and the wisdom to submit to those people. Sharpen my discernment and mold my character until I look and sound more like You.
It is in Jesus name that I pray,
Amen.

CHALLENGE OF THE MONTH

Esther's Deliverance

Generational curses can always be traced back to dishonor! Continue to track and trace the movement of dishonor in your family and renounce it. You are the curse-breaker. Also, find dishonor lurking in your life. Renounce it and start developing new responses, for example, to offense, fear, anger, etc.

ESTHER'S EDICT

Esther's Confession

I am a vessel of honor. I will not participate in dishonor through gossip, slander, rebellion or procrastination. My tongue will speak blessings. My heart will not utter perverse things. Out of my belly shall flow rivers of living water. I am favored and purposed for such a time as this. I will not miss God. I will complete my assignment in the Earth.

ESTHER TRACKER
(Month Four)

This is your journal for the month. List upcoming events, past incidents, your fears, your concerns, your expectations, your hopes, how you intend to respond to the issues you're facing, how you've responded to each issue/incident that you have faced (this month), and how you plan to improve so that you'll be a better woman next month.

If you need more space to write, please use a notebook, but be sure to get it all out.

Before you move on to the journal, please write a note/declaration to yourself (in the box below), detailing how you intend to manage this month.

NOTE TO SELF

Week One

Week Two

Week Three

Week Four

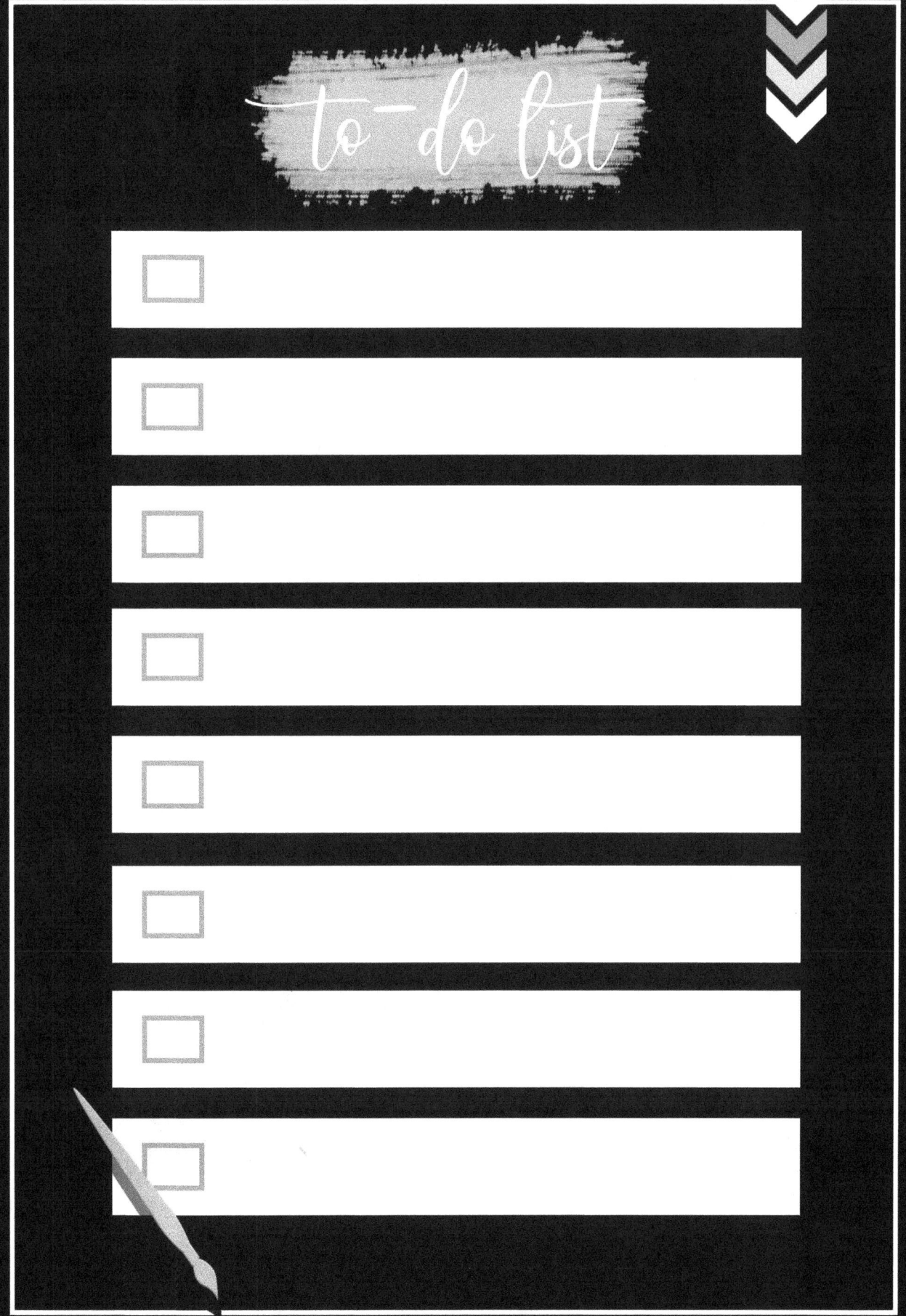

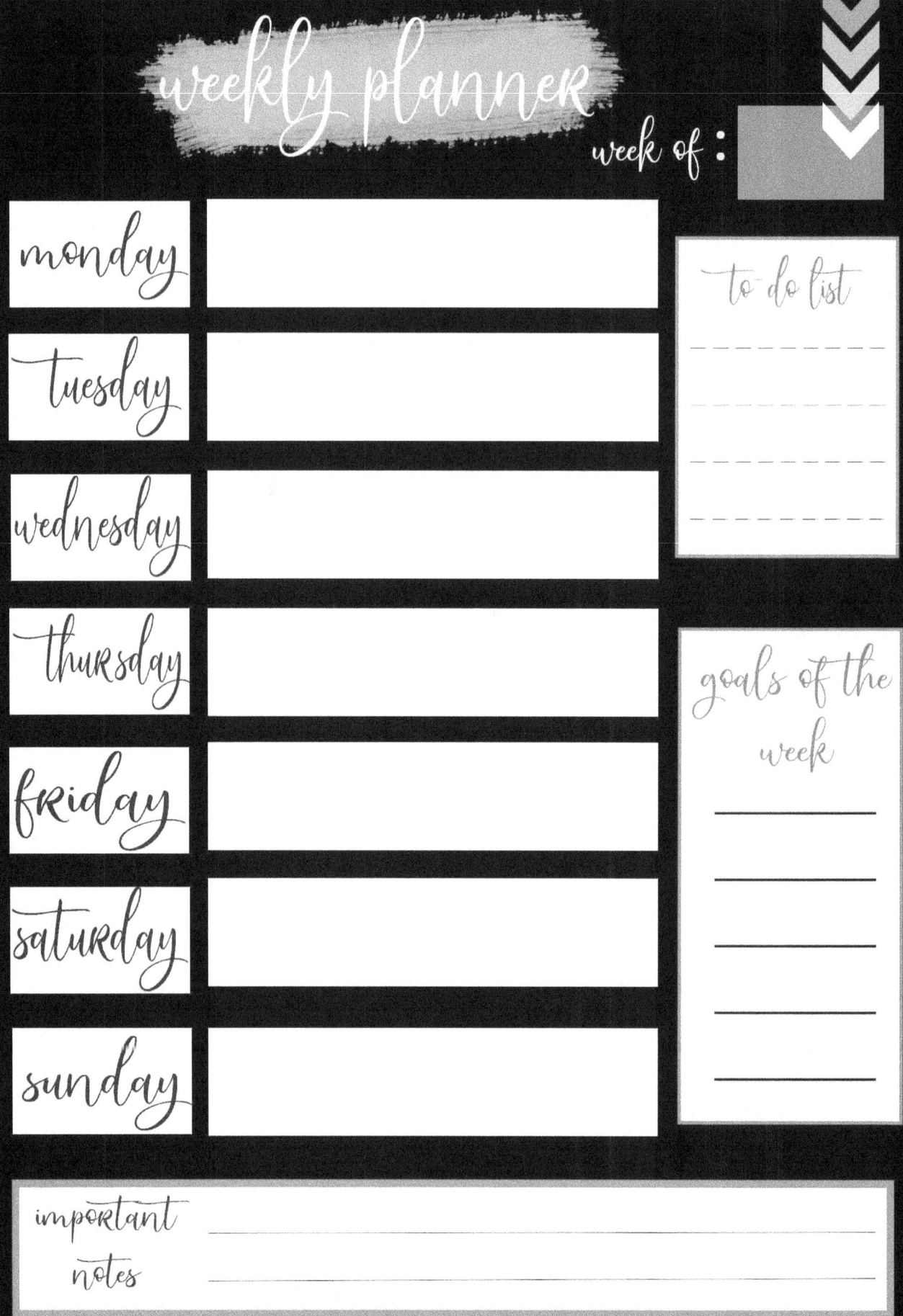

Month Five

The Beauty of Holiness

CROWN JEWEL V

Esther had favor with everyone she came in contact with. Was this because she was beautiful? No. While beauty does open doors, it doesn't keep them open. Vashti was beautiful, but her pride and dishonor caused her to be banished from the throne and cast into utter darkness. What this means is that while the king could not wholly put her away, he could (at minimum) demote her from the position of queen to having the rank, role and rights of a concubine. Howbeit, a part of Vashti's punishment was that the king would never summon her again, which translated to her being locked away in her room, only to surface whenever the concubines went into a common area like the dining hall or out on the yard. She was surrounded by women and eunuchs for the rest of her life. All the same, most (if not all) of the virgins brought before the king were breathtakingly beautiful. But beauty can become a stronghold if the person wearing it begins to trust in it and not God. Howbeit, Esther had favor because she trusted in the Lord and not her reflection. Beauty, when paired with submission, is powerful enough to bring down an entire kingdom. And understand this, favor doesn't have a face. In other words, society doesn't have to reward you with compliments in order for favor to manifest itself as your reality. Favor is oftentimes the product of honor!

HEAVEN'S LOVE LETTER TO YOU

Dear Queen,

Don't be held captive by your reflection. Women who think that doors will open for them because of their physical features are almost always humbled when they spend more time working on their appearance than they do their character. All the same, women who believe themselves to be unattractive are also slaves of their own reflections. These beauties think that doors will shut on them because of their physical features. Consequentially, they are almost always humiliated when they discover that they closed the doors that God opened for them simply because of how they perceived themselves. While man looks at the outward appearance, God looks at the heart, and if your heart is beautiful to Him, He will open doors that man cannot shut. The most beautiful attribute a woman can have in the eyes of the Lord is the beauty of holiness.

Esther 5

On the third day Esther put on her royal robes and stood in the inner court of the king's palace, in front of the king's quarters, while the king was sitting on his royal throne inside the throne room opposite the entrance to the palace. And when the king saw Queen Esther standing in the court, she won favor in his sight, and he held out to Esther the golden scepter that was in his hand. Then Esther approached and touched the tip of the scepter. And the king said to her, "What is it, Queen Esther? What is your request? It shall be given you, even to the half of my kingdom." And Esther said, "If it please the king, let the king and Haman come today to a feast that I have prepared for the king." Then the king said, "Bring Haman quickly, so that we may do as Esther has asked." So the king and Haman came to the feast that Esther had prepared. And as they were drinking wine after the feast, the king said to Esther, "What is your wish? It shall be granted you. And what is your request? Even to the half of my kingdom, it shall be fulfilled." Then Esther answered, "My wish and my request is:

If I have found favor in the sight of the king, and if it please the king to grant my wish and fulfill my request, let the king and Haman come to the feast that I will prepare for them, and tomorrow I will do as the king has said."

And Haman went out that day joyful and glad of heart. But when Haman saw Mordecai in the king's gate, that he neither rose nor trembled before him, he was filled with wrath against Mordecai. Nevertheless, Haman restrained himself and went home, and he sent and brought his friends and his wife Zeresh. And Haman recounted to them the splendor of his riches, the number of his sons, all the promotions with which the king had honored him, and how he had advanced him above the officials and the servants of the king. Then Haman said, "Even Queen Esther let no one but me come with the king to the feast she prepared. And tomorrow also I am invited by her together with the king. Yet all this is worth nothing to me, so long as I see Mordecai the Jew sitting at the king's gate." Then his wife Zeresh and all his friends said to him, "Let a gallows fifty cubits high be made, and in the morning tell the king to have Mordecai hanged upon it. Then go joyfully with the king to the feast." This idea pleased Haman, and he had the gallows made.

WHAT HAVE YOU LEARNED FROM THE SCRIPTURE AND VERSES ABOVE, AND HOW DO YOU PLAN TO APPLY WHAT YOU'VE LEARNED TO YOUR LIFE?

1

2

3

4

5

6

7

8

9

10

11
12
13
14
15

Esther Tracer

(Month Five)

List your fears and other issues, trace them all the way to their roots, and then list what you're going to do to train them. How do you plan to get free? What books are you reading? Who's your therapist? What programs are you in? If you want to grow, heal and be delivered, you have to be intentional and consistent with monitoring and managing your mind.

List Each Fear/ Insecurity/ Issue	Trace Each Fear and Insecurity	Train Each Fear and Insecurity

Esther's Trail

(Month Five)

Any time you participate in any of the events listed below, be sure to pencil in the date. Note, you can write as many dates into one window that you can fit into each space. The goal is to teach you to enjoy your own company.

Event	Dates	Event	Dates
Did Something Nice for Myself		Went to Church	
Dined in Restaurant		Studied Bible	
Exercised		Went to Church	
Encouraged Someone		Studied Bible	
Blessed Someone		Went to Church	
Overcame an Offense		Studied Bible	
Expressed Myself Creatively		Went to Church	
Resisted Temptation		Studied Bible	
Learned Something New		Went to Church	
Broke Cultural Barriers		Studied Bible	
Challenged Myself		Went to Church	

PRAYER CLOSET

Esther's Prayer

Dear Lord,
I put my trust in You and You alone. Set me free from every false god that I have served, and help me to understand what it means to worship You in Spirit and in Truth. Deliver me from the world's systems and every lie that I have adopted as a truth. I present my body, my mind and my spirit to You to be used by You for Your glory. Give me eyes to see and ears to hear what Your Spirit is doing and saying. Let Your name be glorified in and through me.
It is in Jesus name that I pray,
Amen.

CHALLENGE OF THE MONTH

Esther's Deliverance

No more negative self-talk! This month, commit to uplifting yourself and everyone who comes in contact with you. Be extraordinarily positive and pleasant to be around. Prophesy over yourself at least once a day while standing in the mirror or, at minimum, once a week. Cast down, reject and starve all of the lies that you've been told about yourself. Don't allow your reflection to keep you in bondage. Trust in the Lord with all your heart and lean not to your own understanding. In all of your ways, acknowledge Him and He will direct your steps.

ESTHER'S EDICT

Esther's Confession

I am invaluable. I am the answer to somebody's prayers. I will be a light in this world. I will love everyone; yes, even the people who don't love me. Souls will return to Christ because of the love of God that radiates through me. I am a custom created vessel made for the Master's use. I submit myself to the Lord to be used at His discretion.

ESTHER TRACKER
(Month Five)

This is your journal for the month. List upcoming events, past incidents, your fears, your concerns, your expectations, your hopes, how you intend to respond to the issues you're facing, how you've responded to each issue/incident that you have faced (this month), and how you plan to improve so that you'll be a better woman next month.

If you need more space to write, please use a notebook, but be sure to get it all out.

Before you move on to the journal, please write a note/declaration to yourself (in the box below), detailing how you intend to manage this month.

NOTE TO SELF

Week One

Week Two

Week Three

Week Four

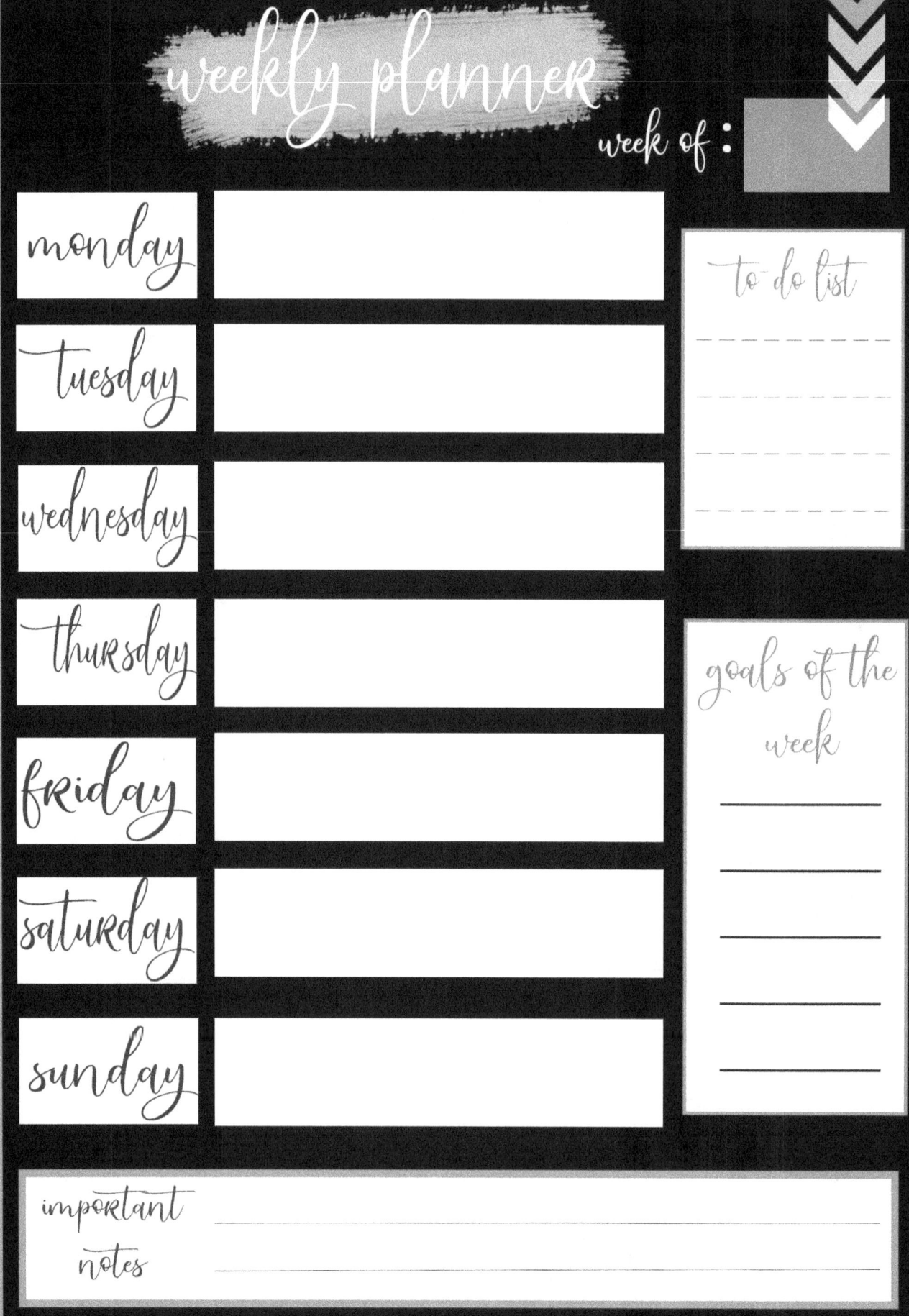

Month Six

Forgive Them and Move On

CROWN JEWEL VI

Forgiveness is one of the jewels in a Queen's crown. It radiates with love, and like a purple heart, it tells a story to onlookers, letting them know that the Queen wearing the crown has not only survived some pretty intense battles, but that she has taken the spoils of war with her.

Forgiveness is not a feeling, it's a decision that you make; yes, even when you can still feel the effects of the heartbreak, disappointment or frustration. It is not something we can do within our own might. Instead, we have to enlist the aid of the Holy Spirit. And whenever we get God involved, He doesn't rewire our emotions, He simply gives us another perspective of the person and the event that broke us. He will take you past the facts and straight to the truth, and from there, you'll be able to see your role in what happened to the adult-sized version of yourself. In other words, He will teach you to take accountability. After all, it may be a fact that your ex cheated on you and left you for another woman, but that's just the fruit of the event. The seed or truth, on the other hand, is that you sinned to get the guy. And while this does not justify what he did to you, it does explain it. If you go into sin, which is a demonic system, you can't expect to come out with an honorable man. Forgiveness helps you to see the event from God's vantage point.

HEAVEN'S LOVE LETTER TO YOU

Dear Queen,
Cry about it, talk about it and be angry about it, but don't forget to pray about it. And most importantly, don't forget to heal, forgive and take the spoils of war (wisdom) with you. Anyone who hurts you is simply communicating with you something that you refused to hear all along. What that person is saying is that he or she cannot serve in the role you've entrusted him or her with. That's okay. Take the lesson and leave that space open until God sends the right person to occupy it.

Esther 6

On that night the king could not sleep. And he gave orders to bring the book of memorable deeds, the chronicles, and they were read before the king. And it was found written how Mordecai had told about Bigthana and Teresh, two of the king's eunuchs, who guarded the threshold, and who had sought to lay hands on King Ahasuerus. And the king said, "What honor or distinction has been bestowed on Mordecai for this?" The king's young men who attended him said, "Nothing has been done for him." And the king said, "Who is in the court?" Now Haman had just entered the outer court of the king's palace to speak to the king about having Mordecai hanged on the gallows that he had prepared for him. And the king's young men told him, "Haman is there, standing in the court." And the king said, "Let him come in." So Haman came in, and the king said to him, "What should be done to the man whom the king delights to honor?" And Haman said to himself, "Whom would the king delight to honor more than me?" And Haman said to the king, "For the man whom the king delights to honor, let royal robes be brought, which the king has worn, and the horse that the king has ridden, and on whose head a royal crown is set. And let the robes and the horse be handed over to one of the king's most noble officials. Let them dress the man whom the king delights to honor, and let them lead him on the horse through the square of the city, proclaiming before him: 'Thus shall it be done to the man whom the king delights to honor.'" Then the king said to Haman, "Hurry; take the robes and the horse, as you have said, and do so to Mordecai the Jew, who sits at the king's gate. Leave out nothing that you have mentioned." So Haman took the robes and the horse, and he dressed Mordecai and led him through the square of the city, proclaiming before him, "Thus shall it be done to the man whom the king delights to honor."

Then Mordecai returned to the king's gate. But Haman hurried to his house, mourning and with his head covered. And Haman told his wife Zeresh and all his friends everything that had happened to him. Then his wise men and his wife Zeresh said to him, "If Mordecai, before whom you have begun to fall, is of the Jewish people, you will not overcome him but will surely fall before him."

While they were yet talking with him, the king's eunuchs arrived and hurried to bring Haman to the feast that Esther had prepared.

What have you learned from the scripture and verses above, and how do you plan to apply what you've learned to your life?

1.

2.

3.

4.

5.

6.

7.

8.

9
10
11
12
13
14
15

Esther Tracer

(Month Six)

List your fears and other issues, trace them all the way to their roots, and then list what you're going to do to train them. How do you plan to get free? What books are you reading? Who's your therapist? What programs are you in? If you want to grow, heal and be delivered, you have to be intentional and consistent with monitoring and managing your mind.

List Each Fear/ Insecurity/ Issue	Trace Each Fear and Insecurity	Train Each Fear and Insecurity

Esther's Trail

(Month Six)

Any time you participate in any of the events listed below, be sure to pencil in the date. Note, you can write as many dates into one window that you can fit into each space. The goal is to teach you to enjoy your own company.

Event	Dates	Event	Dates
Did Something Nice for Myself		Went to Church	
Dined in Restaurant		Studied Bible	
Exercised		Went to Church	
Encouraged Someone		Studied Bible	
Blessed Someone		Went to Church	
Overcame an Offense		Studied Bible	
Expressed Myself Creatively		Went to Church	
Resisted Temptation		Studied Bible	
Learned Something New		Went to Church	
Broke Cultural Barriers		Studied Bible	
Challenged Myself		Went to Church	

PRAYER CLOSET

Esther's Prayer

Dear Lord,
Because of Your unfailing love and grace, You sent Your Son, Jesus Christ, to the Earth to live and die for me so that I could be reconciled to You. I thank You for Your selfless act of love. I thank You that You are Love! Help me to share that same love and grace with others, especially people who have abused, misused and hurt me. Help me to forgive them, and then use me to win as many of them for Your use as possible. Set me free from any and every ungodly soul tie that I have with these people, and don't allow me to be entangled in the yoke of bondage with them ever again.
It is in Jesus name that I pray,
Amen.

CHALLENGE OF THE MONTH

Esther's Deliverance

List the names of the people you've struggled to forgive, and then write a note to each person, releasing them from their debt to you. The note can be as long or as short as you need it to be. Once you're done, pray over the note and ask the Lord to give you His heart towards those people, and then throw the note away. The goal isn't to share the note with the people; it's for you to release yourself from any toxic soul ties that you have with those people.

ESTHER'S EDICT

Esther's Confession

I love my enemies. I decree and declare that every unclean spirit that has ever used them to hurt or harass me is bound and will be cast out at the time appointed. I decree and declare that people will come into their lives who will lead them towards deliverance and healing. What the enemy meant for evil, God is turning around for His glory.

Esther Tracker

(Month Six)

This is your journal for the month. List upcoming events, past incidents, your fears, your concerns, your expectations, your hopes, how you intend to respond to the issues you're facing, how you've responded to each issue/incident that you have faced (this month), and how you plan to improve so that you'll be a better woman next month.

If you need more space to write, please use a notebook, but be sure to get it all out.

Before you move on to the journal, please write a note/declaration to yourself (in the box below), detailing how you intend to manage this month.

Note to Self

Week One

Week Two

Week Three

Week Four

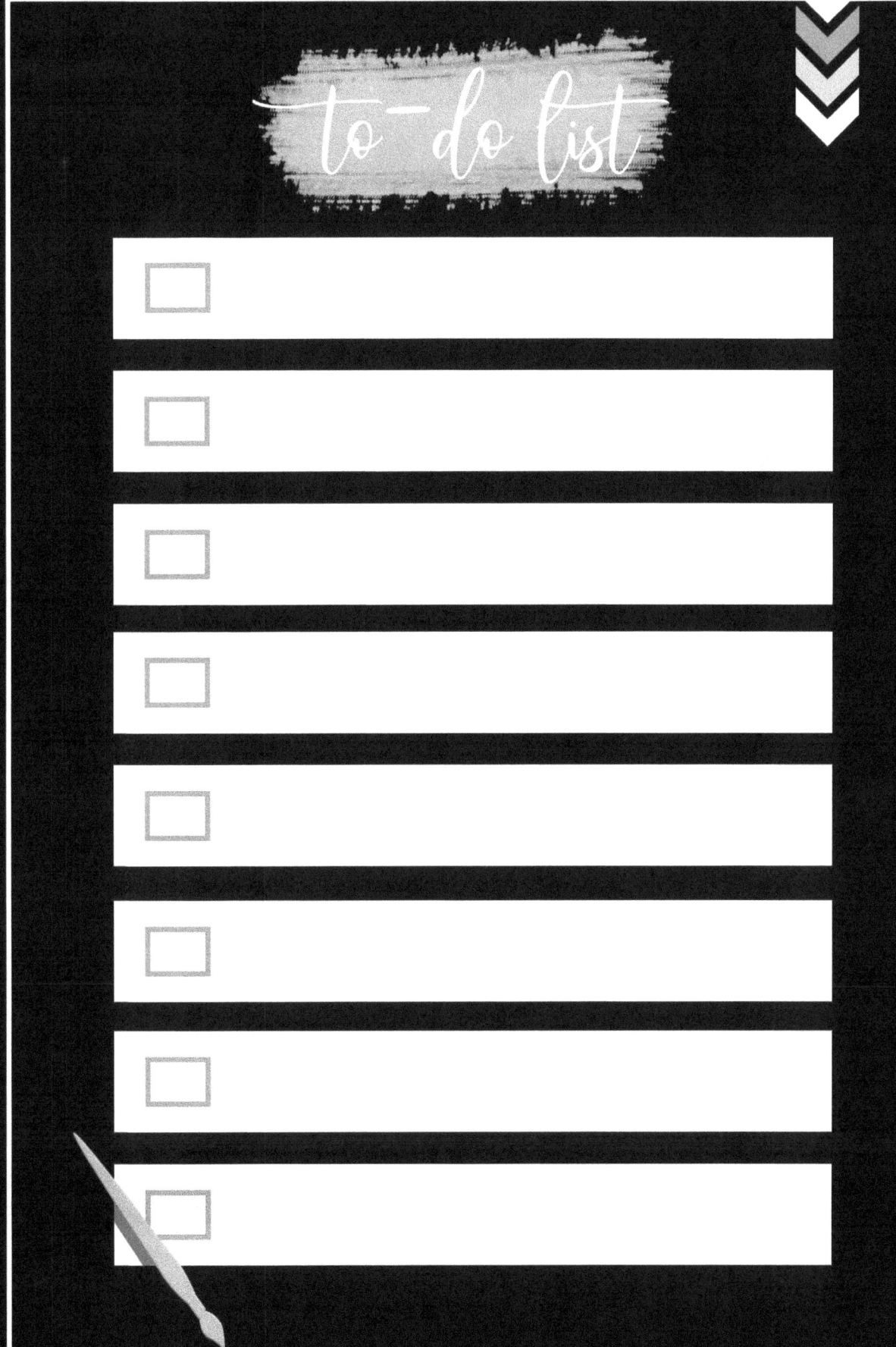

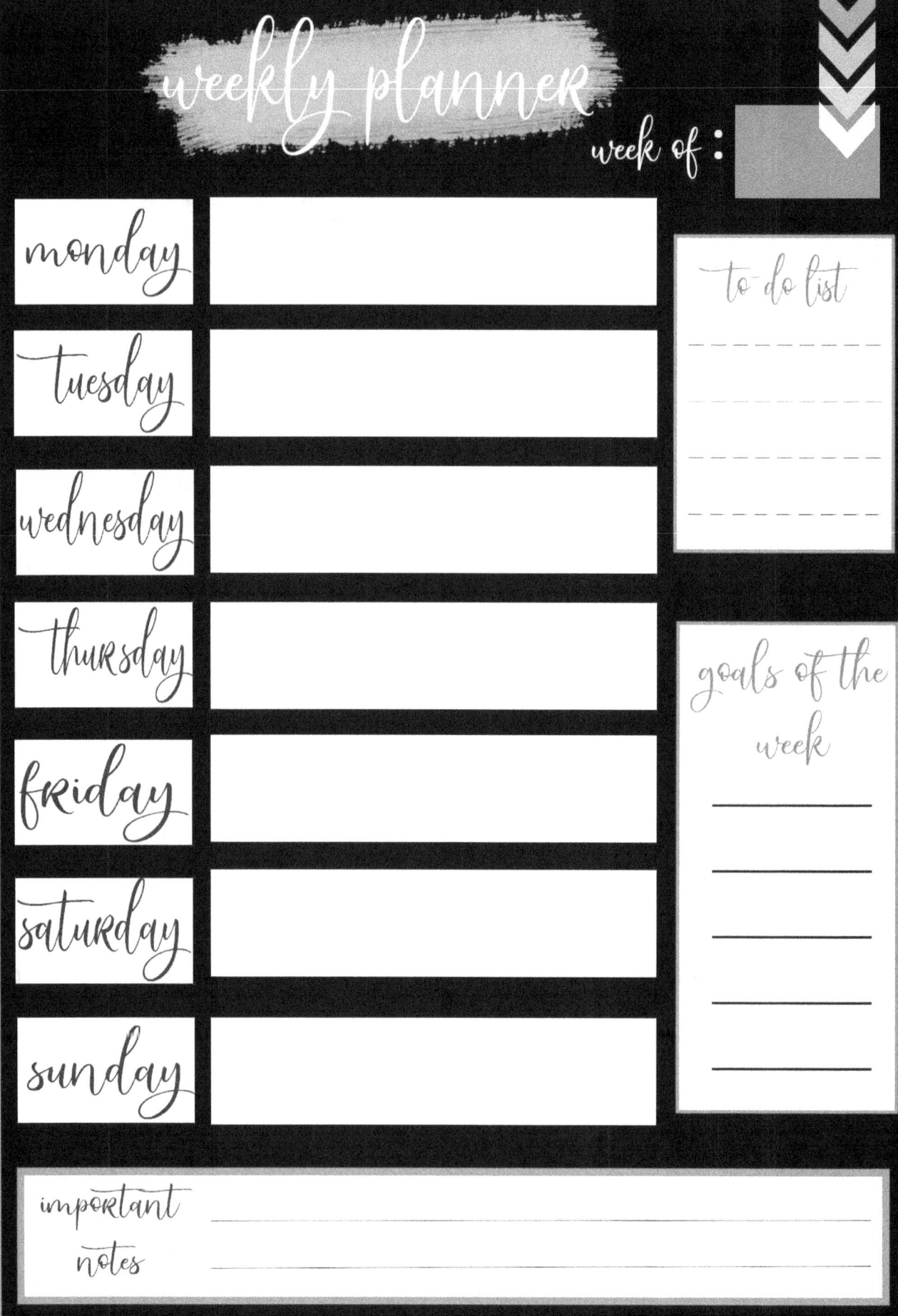

Month Seven

Make Fear Serve You

CROWN JEWEL VII

Enemies or oppositionists are the people God trusts to push us into our rightful positions. Before Haman decided to come against the Jews, Esther had settled into her role as Queen. I'm pretty sure that she thought she'd spend the rest of her life being catered to, but what she didn't realize was that purpose was lurking nearby. She wasn't just the Queen because she was beautiful, she was Queen because she was humble enough to take down a monster like Haman. She fasted, she prayed and she trembled; nevertheless, she had a job to do—one that would cause her to risk her life for her people. Of course, she went before the King and discovered that her favor with him hadn't dissipated. And now, it was time to bring down the King's right-hand man, the second in charge, Haman. Can you imagine the amount of fear, intimidation and anxiety she must've felt in those moments? However, she could not allow fear to shut her mouth. It was time for her to not just be a beautiful fixture sitting inside a castle, it was time for her to tap into the power God had entrusted her with. It was time for her to use her voice.

HEAVEN'S LOVE LETTER TO YOU

Dear Queen,

Fear is a muzzle not fit for a queen. You've been silent long enough, and the enemy interprets your silence as permission to keep ruling in your stead. Dethrone him and take your rightful place. Your voice puts everything and everyone in order and in perspective. Sure, some people may leave your life the minute you take your voice back, but get this, they are simply taking their rightful seats! In other words, your voice will cause the masks to fall off of everyone who dares to wear one in your presence. Your voice is designed to deliver you, but when it's been muzzled, it causes you to yoke yourself up with people who are sent to bind you. I need you to remember this—you are a queen! Act like it! Make fear bow down to you, and not the other way around!

Esther 7

So the king and Haman went in to feast with Queen Esther. And on the second day, as they were drinking wine after the feast, the king again said to Esther, "What is your wish, Queen Esther? It shall be granted you. And what is your request? Even to the half of my kingdom, it shall be fulfilled." Then Queen Esther answered, "If I have found favor in your sight, O king, and if it please the king, let my life be granted me for my wish, and my people for my request. For we have been sold, I and my people, to be destroyed, to be killed, and to be annihilated. If we had been sold merely as slaves, men and women, I would have been silent, for our affliction is not to be compared with the loss to the king." Then King Ahasuerus said to Queen Esther, "Who is he, and where is he, who has dared to do this?" And Esther said, "A foe and enemy! This wicked Haman!" Then Haman was terrified before the king and the queen.

And the king arose in his wrath from the wine-drinking and went into the palace garden, but Haman stayed to beg for his life from Queen Esther, for he saw that harm was determined against him by the king. And the king returned from the palace garden to the place where they were drinking wine, as Haman was falling on the couch where Esther was. And the king said, "Will he even assault the queen in my presence, in my own house?" As the word left the mouth of the king, they covered Haman's face. Then Harbona, one of the eunuchs in attendance on the king, said, "Moreover, the gallows that Haman has prepared for Mordecai, whose word saved the king, is standing at Haman's house, fifty cubits high." And the king said, "Hang him on that." So they hanged Haman on the gallows that he had prepared for Mordecai. Then the wrath of the king abated.

WHAT HAVE YOU LEARNED FROM THE SCRIPTURE AND VERSES ABOVE, AND HOW DO YOU PLAN TO APPLY WHAT YOU'VE LEARNED TO YOUR LIFE?

1

2

3

4

5

6

7

8

9

10

11

12

13	
14	
15	

Esther Tracer

(Month Seven)

List your fears and other issues, trace them all the way to their roots, and then list what you're going to do to train them. How do you plan to get free? What books are you reading? Who's your therapist? What programs are you in? If you want to grow, heal and be delivered, you have to be intentional and consistent with monitoring and managing your mind.

List Each Fear/ Insecurity/ Issue	Trace Each Fear and Insecurity	Train Each Fear and Insecurity

Esther's Trail

(Month Seven)

Any time you participate in any of the events listed below, be sure to pencil in the date. Note, you can write as many dates into one window that you can fit into each space. The goal is to teach you to enjoy your own company.

Event	Dates	Event	Dates
Did Something Nice for Myself		Went to Church	
Dined in Restaurant		Studied Bible	
Exercised		Went to Church	
Encouraged Someone		Studied Bible	
Blessed Someone		Went to Church	
Overcame an Offense		Studied Bible	
Expressed Myself Creatively		Went to Church	
Resisted Temptation		Studied Bible	
Learned Something New		Went to Church	
Broke Cultural Barriers		Studied Bible	
Challenged Myself		Went to Church	

PRAYER CLOSET

Esther's Prayer

Dear Lord,
I will have faith in You. Deliver me from my unbelief! Set me free from fear and everything that entered my life through fear. Restore everything that fear stole from me. Teach me to walk in holy boldness and give me the mind of Christ.
It is in Jesus name that I pray,
Amen.

CHALLENGE OF THE MONTH

Esther's Deliverance

Write a letter to all of your fears renouncing them once and for all. If you don't want to write a letter, write the name of each fear on a piece of paper and renounce it. Also, list an action step; for example, if you fear public speaking, you may decide to record a live video on social media at least once a week until the fear dissipates. You can keep or throw away the letter; that's entirely up to you.

ESTHER'S EDICT

Esther's Confession

Fear is not allowed in my kingdom. I am bold, I am fearless and I am forgiven. The weapons may be formed against me, but they will not prosper. They cannot prosper. I will not fear what man can do to me because God is my strong-tower. In Him, I put my trust. I will not fear the faces of mankind. Fear will not keep me from fulfilling my Kingdom assignment. I walk by faith and not by sight. I have the faith to move mountains. My faith grows everyday.

ESTHER TRACKER

(Month Seven)

This is your journal for the month. List upcoming events, past incidents, your fears, your concerns, your expectations, your hopes, how you intend to respond to the issues you're facing, how you've responded to each issue/incident that you have faced (this month), and how you plan to improve so that you'll be a better woman next month.

If you need more space to write, please use a notebook, but be sure to get it all out.

Before you move on to the journal, please write a note/declaration to yourself (in the box below), detailing how you intend to manage this month.

NOTE TO SELF

Week One

Week Two

Week Three

Week Four

- [ ]
- [ ]
- [ ]
- [ ]
- [ ]
- [ ]
- [ ]
- [ ]

Month Eight

Love Your Enemies

CROWN JEWEL VIII

After your enemies are defeated, it is important that you do not become prideful, boastful or arrogant. This is oftentimes the test that most Queens fail, especially those who haven't fully forgiven the people who rejected, mishandled, abandoned or persecuted them. Nowadays, you can see unforgiveness manifesting itself all over social media. When a broken person gets a snapshot or a snippet of a blessing, that person allows hurt and bitterness to guide his or her response. Consequently, we see women posting up pictures of their victories with captions that read, for example, "They thought they could hold me back, but God still turned around and gave me another victory! Cheers to my haters!" Posts like these wreak of unforgiveness, narcissism and pride. Other hate-laced posts include ones that mock the people who the poster feels are against her, especially when those people are facing a calamity. How does God respond? Proverbs 24:18 reads, "Do not rejoice when your enemy falls, and let not your heart be glad when he stumbles, lest the Lord see it and be displeased, and turn away his anger from him."

Queens don't mock or mishandle the people who hurt them. Instead, we behave like royalty so that we can give God the glory, even in the midst of our enemies.

HEAVEN'S LOVE LETTER TO YOU

Dear Queen,

Psalm 23:5 reads, "Thou preparest a table before me in the presence of mine enemies: thou anointest my head with oil; my cup runneth over." Of course, this was one of King David's poetic journal entries. Psalm 23:5 has become the national anthem for unforgiving saints. What they don't realize, however, is that they've taken the text out of context.

Think about a huge banquet hall. Inside of this hall is a long table, and at the head of the table is a throne set in place for God. At the other end of the table, is a throne set in place for you. The seats around the table all represent people who have or had access to you on some level. To your left are your enemies. To your right are those who've supported and loved you. If God were to physically set a situation like this in motion, why do you think He'd place your enemies at the same table? It's not to humiliate them. It's because He loves them and wants to deliver them, but if you think it's for you to mock them and further provoke their jealousy, you'll allow yourself to be an instrument that Satan uses to hurt, harass and humiliate them all the more. Queen, pray for them who spitefully use you. Sometimes, the greatest evangelistic opportunities that you'll have will come while you're being honored in the midst of people who'd rather see you humiliated.

Esther 8

On that day King Ahasuerus gave to Queen Esther the house of Haman, the enemy of the Jews. And Mordecai came before the king, for Esther had told what he was to her. And the king took off his signet ring, which he had taken from Haman, and gave it to Mordecai. And Esther set Mordecai over the house of Haman.

Then Esther spoke again to the king. She fell at his feet and wept and pleaded with him to avert the evil plan of Haman the Agagite and the plot that he had devised against the Jews. When the king held out the golden scepter to Esther, Esther rose and stood before the king. And she said, "If it please the king, and if I have found favor in his sight, and if the thing seems right before the king, and I am pleasing in his eyes, let an order be written to revoke the letters devised by Haman the Agagite, the son of Hammedatha, which he wrote to destroy the Jews who are in all the provinces of the king. For how can I bear to see the calamity that is coming to my people? Or how can I bear to see the destruction of my kindred?" Then King Ahasuerus said to Queen Esther and to Mordecai the Jew, "Behold, I have given Esther the house of Haman, and they have hanged him on the gallows, because he intended to lay hands on the Jews. But you may write as you please with regard to the Jews, in the name of the king, and seal it with the king's ring, for an edict written in the name of the king and sealed with the king's ring cannot be revoked."

The king's scribes were summoned at that time, in the third month, which is the month of Sivan, on the twenty-third day. And an edict was written, according to all that Mordecai commanded concerning the Jews, to the satraps and the governors and the officials of the provinces from India to Ethiopia, 127 provinces, to each province in its own script and to each people in its own language, and also to the Jews in their script and their language. And he wrote in the name of King Ahasuerus and sealed it with the king's signet ring. Then he sent the letters by mounted couriers riding on swift horses that were used in the king's service, bred from the royal stud, saying that the king allowed the Jews who were in every city to gather and defend their lives, to destroy, to kill, and to annihilate any armed force of any people or province that might attack them, children and women included, and to plunder their goods, on one day throughout all the provinces of King Ahasuerus, on the thirteenth day of the twelfth month, which is the month of Adar. A copy of what was written was to be issued as a decree in every province, being publicly displayed to all peoples, and the Jews were to be ready on that day to take vengeance on their enemies. So the couriers, mounted on their swift horses that were used in the king's service, rode out hurriedly, urged by the king's command. And the decree was issued in Susa the citadel.

Then Mordecai went out from the presence of the king in royal robes of blue and white, with a great golden crown and a robe of fine linen and purple, and the city of Susa shouted and rejoiced. The Jews had light and gladness and joy and honor. And in every province and in every city, wherever the king's command and his edict reached, there was gladness and joy among the Jews, a feast and a holiday. And many from the peoples of the country declared themselves Jews, for fear of the Jews had fallen on them.

WHAT HAVE YOU LEARNED FROM THE SCRIPTURE AND VERSES ABOVE, AND HOW DO YOU PLAN TO APPLY WHAT YOU'VE LEARNED TO YOUR LIFE?

1

2

3

4

5

6

7

8

9

10

11

12

13

14

15

ESTHER TRACER

(Month Eight)

List your fears and other issues, trace them all the way to their roots, and then list what you're going to do to train them. How do you plan to get free? What books are you reading? Who's your therapist? What programs are you in? If you want to grow, heal and be delivered, you have to be intentional and consistent with monitoring and managing your mind.

List Each Fear/ Insecurity/ Issue	Trace Each Fear and Insecurity	Train Each Fear and Insecurity

Esther's Trail

(Month Eight)

Any time you participate in any of the events listed below, be sure to pencil in the date. Note, you can write as many dates into one window that you can fit into each space. The goal is to teach you to enjoy your own company.

Event	Dates	Event	Dates
Did Something Nice for Myself		Went to Church	
Dined in Restaurant		Studied Bible	
Exercised		Went to Church	
Encouraged Someone		Studied Bible	
Blessed Someone		Went to Church	
Overcame an Offense		Studied Bible	
Expressed Myself Creatively		Went to Church	
Resisted Temptation		Studied Bible	
Learned Something New		Went to Church	
Broke Cultural Barriers		Studied Bible	
Challenged Myself		Went to Church	

PRAYER CLOSET

Esther's Prayer

Dear Lord,
Deliver me from my enemies. Do not allow them to have victory over me. Instead, let Your love radiate through me so that they can know, understand and receive Your love and embrace Your salvation. Let the words that they speak against me fall to the ground. Let the weapons that they form against me turn into dust. In the midst of it all, let them witness Your relentless love towards me and your unwavering love towards them. Let them thirst and hunger for righteousness, and if they cry out to You, let them be filled. Rescue, deliver and use them for Your glory.
It is in Jesus name that I pray,
Amen.

CHALLENGE OF THE MONTH

Esther's Deliverance

Plant a garden and watch it grow. In this garden, you are growing the fruits of the Holy Spirit. Demonstrate each and every one of them everyday so that they can mature. Renounce the works of the flesh, and whenever you find yourself operating in one of these works, repent and counter that work by blessing someone, especially one of your enemies.

ESTHER'S EDICT

Esther's Confession

I choose love over hate, faith over fear and peace over conflict. I will demonstrate love, especially when my enemies surround me. I won't just be loving, but I will manifest myself as love, a living vessel filled with the character and essence of God. I will not allow pride to talk me out of loving others. I choose love.

ESTHER TRACKER
(Month Eight)

This is your journal for the month. List upcoming events, past incidents, your fears, your concerns, your expectations, your hopes, how you intend to respond to the issues you're facing, how you've responded to each issue/incident that you have faced (this month), and how you plan to improve so that you'll be a better woman next month.

If you need more space to write, please use a notebook, but be sure to get it all out.

Before you move on to the journal, please write a note/declaration to yourself (in the box below), detailing how you intend to manage this month.

Note to Self

Week One

Week Two

Week Three

Week Four

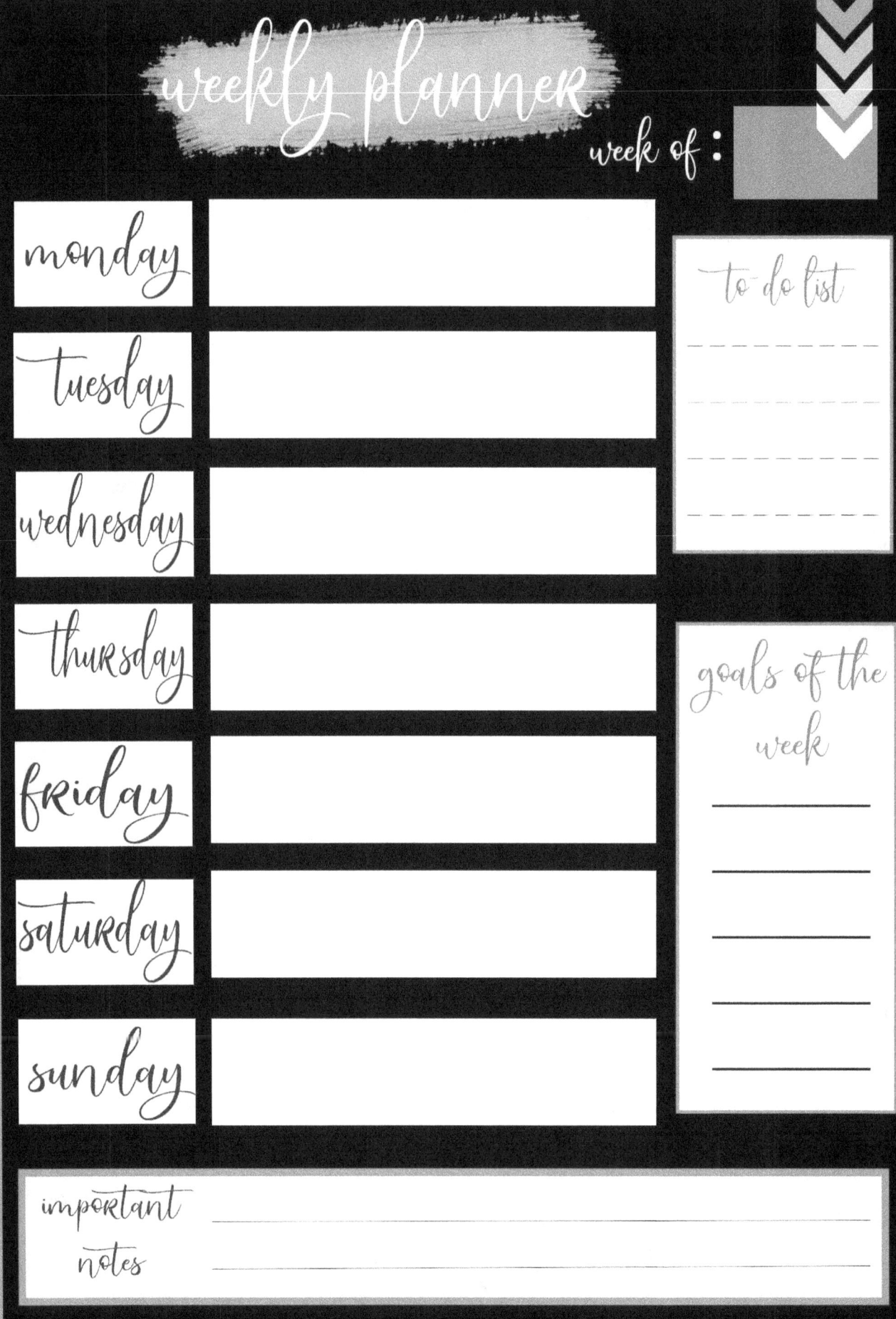

Month Nine

Conquer, but Don't Forget to Heal

CROWN JEWEL IX

There is a season for everything underneath the sun, including healing. A lot of women overcome their goliaths, but in their haste to celebrate their victories, they forget to heal. Consequently, their Goliaths continue to control them, even though they've been defeated. These women become bitter, unforgiving and ambitious, but their thirst for success is driven by their pain. This only causes them to attract more Goliaths; this is because predators are attracted to prey. People who see themselves as victims, by default, will attract victimizers or offenders. To defeat this, they must heal and allow the Lord to change their perspectives. We are more than conquerors in Christ Jesus! We can't just say this, we have to live it!

HEAVEN'S LOVE LETTER TO YOU

Dear Queen,

You've won, but the battle isn't over. Now, you need to heal. Healing doesn't come over time, numbness does. But if you truly want to heal, you have to do the work needed. For example, it's a great idea to seek therapy whenever the pain is too much to bear or when the pain/offense outstays its welcome.

For every process you find yourself in, including the healing process, don't rush the results. Respect the process and allow God to not only heal you, but to educate you about the storm that you just came out of. This is how you ensure that you won't return to the vomit that God pulled you away from.

Esther 9

Now in the twelfth month, which is the month of Adar, on the thirteenth day of the same, when the king's command and edict were about to be carried out, on the very day when the enemies of the Jews hoped to gain the mastery over them, the reverse occurred: the Jews gained mastery over those who hated them. The Jews gathered in their cities throughout all the provinces of King Ahasuerus to lay hands on those who sought their harm. And no one could stand against them, for the fear of them had fallen on all peoples. All the officials of the provinces and the satraps and the governors and the royal agents also helped the Jews, for the fear of Mordecai had fallen on them. For Mordecai was great in the king's house, and his fame spread throughout all the provinces, for the man Mordecai grew more and more powerful. The Jews struck all their enemies with the sword, killing and destroying them, and did as they pleased to those who hated them. In Susa the citadel itself the Jews killed and destroyed 500 men, and also killed Parshandatha and Dalphon and Aspatha and Poratha and Adalia and Aridatha and Parmashta and Arisai and Aridai and Vaizatha, the ten sons of Haman the son of Hammedatha, the enemy of the Jews, but they laid no hand on the plunder.

That very day the number of those killed in Susa the citadel was reported to the king. And the king said to Queen Esther, "In Susa the citadel the Jews have killed and destroyed 500 men and also the ten sons of Haman. What then have they done in the rest of the king's provinces! Now what is your wish? It shall be granted you. And what further is your request? It shall be fulfilled." And Esther said, "If it please the king, let the Jews who are in Susa be allowed tomorrow also to do according to this day's edict. And let the ten sons of Haman be hanged on the gallows." So the king commanded this to be done. A decree was issued in Susa, and the ten sons of Haman were hanged. The Jews who were in Susa gathered also on the fourteenth day of the month of Adar and they killed 300 men in Susa, but they laid no hands on the plunder.

Now the rest of the Jews who were in the king's provinces also gathered to defend their lives, and got relief from their enemies and killed 75,000 of those who hated them, but they laid no hands on the plunder. This was on the thirteenth day of the month of Adar, and on the fourteenth day they rested and made that a day of feasting and gladness. But the Jews who were in Susa gathered on the thirteenth day and on the fourteenth, and rested on the fifteenth day, making that a day of feasting and gladness. Therefore the Jews of the villages, who live in the rural towns, hold the fourteenth day of the month of Adar as a day for gladness and feasting, as a holiday, and as a day on which they send gifts of food to one another.

And Mordecai recorded these things and sent letters to all the Jews who were in all the provinces of King Ahasuerus, both near and far, obliging them to keep the fourteenth day of the month Adar and also the fifteenth day of the same, year by year, as the days on which the Jews *got relief from their enemies, and as the month that had been turned for them from sorrow into gladness and from mourning into a holiday; that they should make them days of feasting and gladness, days for sending gifts of food to one another and gifts to the poor.*

So the Jews accepted what they had started to do, and what Mordecai had written to them. For Haman the Agagite, the son of Hammedatha, the enemy of all the Jews, had plotted against the Jews to destroy them, and had cast Pur (that is, cast lots), to crush and to destroy them. But when it came before the king, he gave orders in writing that his evil plan that he had devised against the Jews should return on his own head, and that he and his sons should be hanged on the gallows. Therefore they called these days Purim, after the term Pur. Therefore, because of all that was written in this letter, and of what they had faced in this matter, and of what had happened to them, the Jews firmly obligated themselves and their offspring and all who joined them, that without fail they would keep these two days according to what was written and at the time appointed every year, that these days should be remembered and kept throughout every generation, in every clan, province, and city, and that these days of Purim should never fall into disuse among the Jews, nor should the commemoration of these days cease among their descendants.

Then Queen Esther, the daughter of Abihail, and Mordecai the Jew gave full written authority, confirming this second letter about Purim. Letters were sent to all the Jews, to the 127 provinces of the kingdom of Ahasuerus, in words of peace and truth, that these days of Purim should be observed at their appointed seasons, as Mordecai the Jew and Queen Esther obligated them, and as they had obligated themselves and their offspring, with regard to their fasts and their lamenting. The command of Esther confirmed these practices of Purim, and it was recorded in writing.

WHAT HAVE YOU LEARNED FROM THE SCRIPTURE AND VERSES ABOVE, AND HOW DO YOU PLAN TO APPLY WHAT YOU'VE LEARNED TO YOUR LIFE?

1	
2	

3
4
5
6
7
8
9
10
11

12

13

14

15

Esther Tracer

(Month Nine)

List your fears and other issues, trace them all the way to their roots, and then list what you're going to do to train them. How do you plan to get free? What books are you reading? Who's your therapist? What programs are you in? If you want to grow, heal and be delivered, you have to be intentional and consistent with monitoring and managing your mind.

List Each Fear/ Insecurity/ Issue	Trace Each Fear and Insecurity	Train Each Fear and Insecurity

Esther's Trail

(Month Nine)

Any time you participate in any of the events listed below, be sure to pencil in the date. Note, you can write as many dates into one window that you can fit into each space. The goal is to teach you to enjoy your own company.

Event	Dates	Event	Dates
Did Something Nice for Myself		Went to Church	
Dined in Restaurant		Studied Bible	
Exercised		Went to Church	
Encouraged Someone		Studied Bible	
Blessed Someone		Went to Church	
Overcame an Offense		Studied Bible	
Expressed Myself Creatively		Went to Church	
Resisted Temptation		Studied Bible	
Learned Something New		Went to Church	
Broke Cultural Barriers		Studied Bible	
Challenged Myself		Went to Church	

PRAYER CLOSET

Esther's Prayer

Dear Lord,
My heart has suffered through a lot. I have had times when I wanted to give up, but You kept me. Thank you for who You are. I ask that You heal me from the inside out. Heal me of my traumas. Heal my hidden wounds. Fill my voids with Your love and revelation. Empty me of all demonic residue, and give me a fresh in-filling of Your Holy Spirit.
It is in Jesus name that I pray,
Amen.

CHALLENGE OF THE MONTH

Esther's Deliverance

Record a video detailing some of the hurts you've been through, and how God healed you of those traumas. Make sure the video is recorded and edited in excellence because it could potentially go viral! This means that you are to post that video PUBLICLY. If you are not ready to fulfill this challenge, skip over it for now, but be sure to do it within the next month or two. Freedom means coming outside your comfort zone so that you can free others. Remember, it's not about you; God wants you to help and heal others as well.

ESTHER'S EDICT

Esther's Confession

I am healed of my past traumas. I am whole. I command the enemy to loose everything he stole from me when he decided to attack me and my bloodline. I spoil the enemy's camp. Healing is my portion. Deliverance is my portion. And the wealth of the wicked is laid up for me. I command that it be released to me now! The healing balm of Gilead is upon me. I am healed, I am free and I am wise.

ESTHER TRACKER
(Month Nine)

This is your journal for the month. List upcoming events, past incidents, your fears, your concerns, your expectations, your hopes, how you intend to respond to the issues you're facing, how you've responded to each issue/incident that you have faced (this month), and how you plan to improve so that you'll be a better woman next month.

If you need more space to write, please use a notebook, but be sure to get it all out.

Before you move on to the journal, please write a note/declaration to yourself (in the box below), detailing how you intend to manage this month.

NOTE TO SELF

Week One

Week Two

Week Three

Week Four

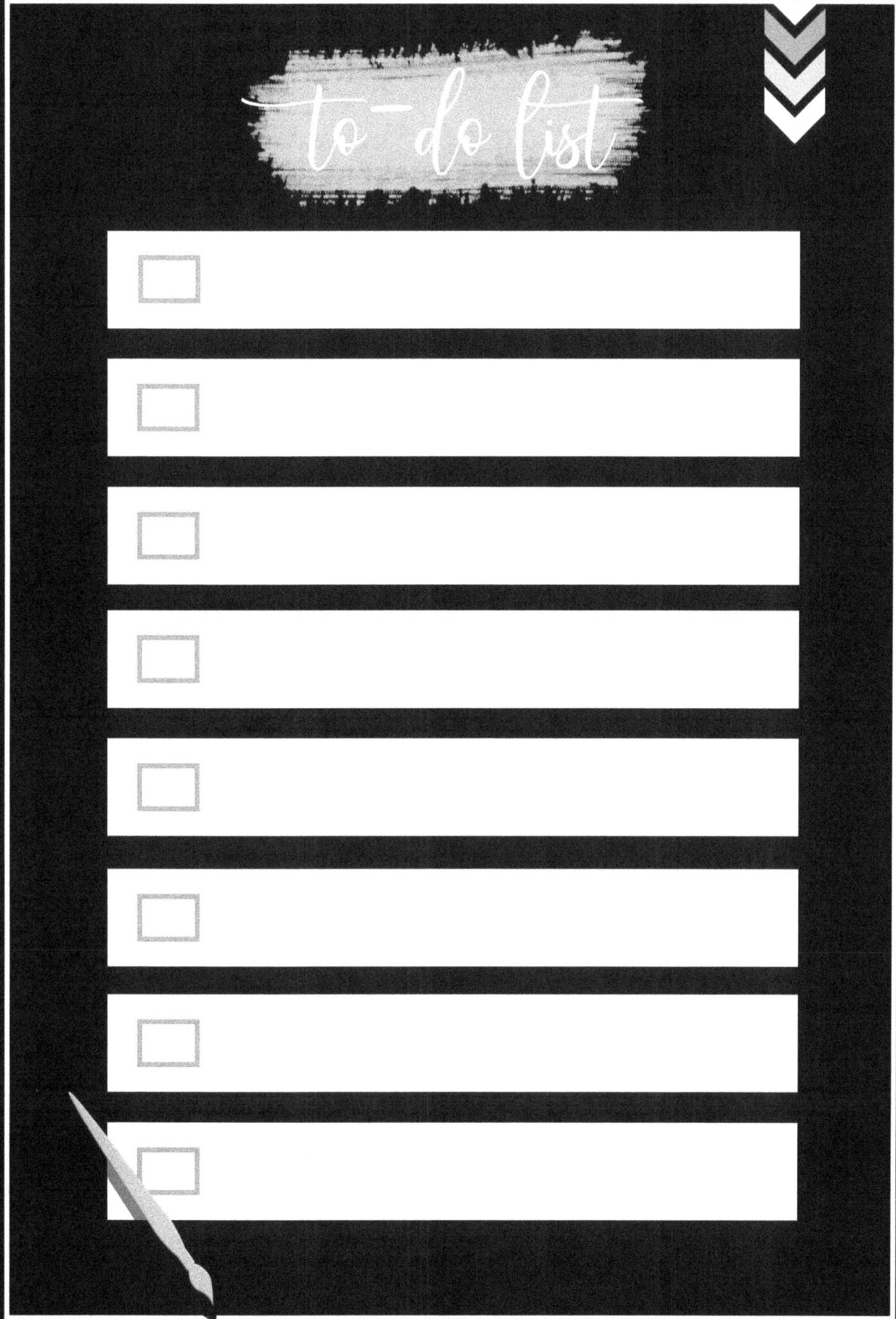

weekly planner

week of:

- monday
- tuesday
- wednesday
- thursday
- friday
- saturday
- sunday

to do list

goals of the week

important notes

Month Ten

The Great Falling Away

CROWN JEWEL X

One of the most humbling events any Queen can endure is the loss of a friend. Right now, you've probably looked around and noticed that many of the people who once graced you with their presence are no longer a part of your inner court. Your phone doesn't ring as much as it used to, and somehow you sense that there are a lot of people out there waiting on you to fail and to fall.

"Someone needs to knock her off her high-horse!"
"What goes up must come down!"
"She thinks she's better than everyone!"
"The higher you climb, the bigger the fall!"

This is the language of the "left behind." These are the rantings of the proverbial "crabs in a bucket"—People who are upset because you got blessed outside of their influence or their permission. They'd written you off, and when you started ascending, they'd tried to sabotage you, but to no avail. Finally, they thought that withholding their support from you would discourage you enough to where you'd give up, but it didn't work. And now, they are watching your life closely, hoping to see you fall. Nevertheless, as long as you stay in Christ, He will continue to lift you up, but remember, this isn't to harass or hurt them. He wants to save them.

When the wrong people walk out of your life, they're simply making room for the right ones.

HEAVEN'S LOVE LETTER TO YOU

Dear Queen,

Every woman who dares to ascend the heights of maturity and success can attest to the fact that their inner circle looks nothing like it did when they first started their journeys. As you grow, as you heal and as you build, many of the people closest to you will begin to fall away, and sometimes, the smallest offenses will chase away those closest to you. One of the keys to ascension is this—you have to let them go to grow! And more importantly, you have to forgive them. No worries. God will bring better friends and people your way; these are people who will not only celebrate your promotions, but these Queens will also open doors for you, just as you do for them. It's okay to mourn the failed friendships, but just don't stay there and definitely, don't become bitter!

Esther 10

King Ahasuerus imposed tax on the land and on the coastlands of the sea. And all the acts of his power and might, and the full account of the high honor of Mordecai, to which the king advanced him, are they not written in the Book of the Chronicles of the kings of Media and Persia? For Mordecai the Jew was second in rank to King Ahasuerus, and he was great among the Jews and popular with the multitude of his brothers, for he sought the welfare of his people and spoke peace to all his people.

WHAT HAVE YOU LEARNED FROM THE SCRIPTURE AND VERSES ABOVE, AND HOW DO YOU PLAN TO APPLY WHAT YOU'VE LEARNED TO YOUR LIFE?

1	
2	
3	
4	
5	
6	

| 7 |
| 8 |
| 9 |
| 10 |
| 11 |
| 12 |
| 13 |
| 14 |
| 15 |

Esther Tracer
(Month Ten)

List your fears and other issues, trace them all the way to their roots, and then list what you're going to do to train them. How do you plan to get free? What books are you reading? Who's your therapist? What programs are you in? If you want to grow, heal and be delivered, you have to be intentional and consistent with monitoring and managing your mind.

List Each Fear/ Insecurity/ Issue	Trace Each Fear and Insecurity	Train Each Fear and Insecurity

Esther's Trail

(Month Ten)

Any time you participate in any of the events listed below, be sure to pencil in the date. Note, you can write as many dates into one window that you can fit into each space. The goal is to teach you to enjoy your own company.

Event	Dates	Event	Dates
Did Something Nice for Myself		Went to Church	
Dined in Restaurant		Studied Bible	
Exercised		Went to Church	
Encouraged Someone		Studied Bible	
Blessed Someone		Went to Church	
Overcame an Offense		Studied Bible	
Expressed Myself Creatively		Went to Church	
Resisted Temptation		Studied Bible	
Learned Something New		Went to Church	
Broke Cultural Barriers		Studied Bible	
Challenged Myself		Went to Church	

PRAYER CLOSET

Esther's Prayer

Dear Lord,
Thank you for every covenant relationship that you've brought me into. I ask that You deliver me from false covenants. I ask that You remove every person from my life who You don't want in it, and give me peace with letting them go. I ask that You send the right people in my life, and give me the wisdom that I need to love and honor them. And for every person who You allow to remain in my life, please give them their rightful places. Don't allow me to assign them to roles that they are not mature or healed enough to hold. Give me wisdom in relationships.
It is in Jesus name that I pray,
Amen.

CHALLENGE OF THE MONTH

Esther's Deliverance

List the names of every person who has an active seat in your life. If it's more than twenty people, list the top ten. Reevaluate their roles in your life and your roles in their lives. Are they too close (they keep hurting you) or are they too far (they keep trying to help you)? Are they expecting too much from you? Are they holding you back or pushing you forward? Rearrange your relationships by looking at the fruits that manifest in those relationships. Be sure to pray and ask the Holy Spirit to assist you.

ESTHER'S EDICT

Esther's Confession

I am kind. I will show myself friendly. I am wise. I am discerning. I will not allow loneliness and rejection to pick my friends for me. I am a blessing to those around me, and I forgive everyone who walks away from me. My covenant relationships are healthy. My mind is healthy. My heart is healthy. My soul is healthy.

ESTHER TRACKER
(Month Ten)

This is your journal for the month. List upcoming events, past incidents, your fears, your concerns, your expectations, your hopes, how you intend to respond to the issues you're facing, how you've responded to each issue/incident that you have faced (this month), and how you plan to improve so that you'll be a better woman next month.

If you need more space to write, please use a notebook, but be sure to get it all out.

Before you move on to the journal, please write a note/declaration to yourself (in the box below), detailing how you intend to manage this month.

NOTE TO SELF

Week One

Week Two

Week Three

Week Four

Month Eleven

You're a Queen, Not a Concubine

CROWN JEWEL XI

Fact: Many kings, both Jewish and Gentile, had hundreds if not thousands of concubines. How on earth did one king satisfy all of those women? He didn't and he couldn't! What most people don't realize is that once a king united himself to a woman in marriage, it was common for that woman to have one night with the king, never to see him up close and personal again. It was only if she pleased the king that he would remember her. Most women would be taken to the concubines' chambers where they'd remain for the rest of their lives. The only time they'd be summoned again was if the king remembered them or he happened to see them, for example, out on the yard or in a common area. They couldn't divorce the king or be with another man, so if they didn't get pregnant during their first encounter with the king, they could potentially go the rest of their lives not knowing what it was like to be mothers. This is to say that being a king's wife or concubine wasn't necessarily the fairy tale that disney has made it out to be. Nevertheless, it was still considered to be a privilege and an honor to be part of a king's harem.

It is possible that the king spotted some of these young women years after he'd married them, maybe out in the yard. He would then inquire of them, asking his eunuchs who a specific girl was, and then requesting that she be sent into his room that night. After that event, she could potentially never be summoned again or the king could summon her months or years later. Of course, most women in the King's harem wanted to give birth to his children, especially his sons, so they went out of their way to ensure that the nights they'd spent with him were memorable, at least on his part.

HEAVEN'S LOVE LETTER TO YOU

Dear Queen,

Men don't normally "end" their relationships with (good) women. In truth, they end their "up close and personal" dealings with women, but for the most part, the majority of men walk away from relationships when they are immature and unsure. In other words, they want to "sow their royal oats." Most women serving as "exes" are completely unaware of this truth, and because of this, they are often flattered when the men from their pasts suddenly start texting, inboxing or calling them out of the blue. But dear Queen, this is nothing to be flattered about. Immature men see women as property. In other words, they see their exes as a part of their personalized harems, and whenever they remember an ex, they summon her with a "Good morning," text or a "Just checking on you to see how you're doing" call. You are a Queen, not a concubine. This is why you shouldn't entertain men who've discounted you in their minds. And get this, it is possible for a man to have a woman serving in a main role in his life, only for him to demote her to the status of a concubine once he comes across someone he feels is better suited for the main role.

The point is, most men don't walk away from good women. They simply (attempt to) transition the roles that the women serve in, but because concubinage is not commonplace or accepted in the western world and many countries influenced by the western world, they have to transition those roles by simply calling for an end to the relationship. Many of the women in the biblical days didn't have a choice or a voice; they had to serve in the roles that they'd been crowned with, but you, oh Queen, do not have to settle for a lesser seat. Don't let some man decorate a toilet, call it a throne and convince you to sit on it.

Matthew 25:1-13

"Then the kingdom of heaven will be like ten virgins who took their lamps and went to meet the bridegroom. Five of them were foolish, and five were wise. For when the foolish took their lamps, they took no oil with them, but the wise took flasks of oil with their lamps. As the bridegroom was delayed, they all became drowsy and slept. But at midnight there was a cry, 'Here is the bridegroom! Come out to meet him.' Then all those virgins rose and trimmed their lamps. And the foolish said to the wise, 'Give us some of your oil, for our lamps are going out.' But the wise answered, saying, 'Since there will not be enough for us and for you, go rather to the dealers and buy for yourselves.' And while they were going to buy, the bridegroom came, and those who were ready went in with him to the marriage feast, and the door was shut. Afterward the other virgins came also, saying, 'Lord, lord, open to us.' But he answered, 'Truly, I say to you, I do not know you.' Watch therefore, for you know neither the day nor the hour.

WHAT HAVE YOU LEARNED FROM THE SCRIPTURE AND VERSES ABOVE, AND HOW DO YOU PLAN TO APPLY WHAT YOU'VE LEARNED TO YOUR LIFE?

1.

2.

3.

4.

5.

6

7

8

9

10

11

12

13

14

Esther Tracer

(Month Eleven)

List your fears and other issues, trace them all the way to their roots, and then list what you're going to do to train them. How do you plan to get free? What books are you reading? Who's your therapist? What programs are you in? If you want to grow, heal and be delivered, you have to be intentional and consistent with monitoring and managing your mind.

List Each Fear/ Insecurity/ Issue	Trace Each Fear and Insecurity	Train Each Fear and Insecurity

ESTHER'S TRAIL

(Month Eleven)

Any time you participate in any of the events listed below, be sure to pencil in the date. Note, you can write as many dates into one window that you can fit into each space. The goal is to teach you to enjoy your own company.

Event	Dates	Event	Dates
Did Something Nice for Myself		Went to Church	
Dined in Restaurant		Studied Bible	
Exercised		Went to Church	
Encouraged Someone		Studied Bible	
Blessed Someone		Went to Church	
Overcame an Offense		Studied Bible	
Expressed Myself Creatively		Went to Church	
Resisted Temptation		Studied Bible	
Learned Something New		Went to Church	
Broke Cultural Barriers		Studied Bible	
Challenged Myself		Went to Church	

PRAYER CLOSET

Esther's Prayer

Dear Lord,

Thank You for loving, healing and forgiving me. Thank You for Your Son, Christ Yeshua. Lord, I ask that You sever every ungodly soul tie that I am a part of. Set me free from the mind of a concubine, and give me the mind of Christ. Teach me to think, live and reason as an honorable daughter of Yours, and grow me up so that I can serve as a healed, happy and purposeful wife to whatever man You release me to.

It is in Jesus name that I pray,

Amen.

CHALLENGE OF THE MONTH

Esther's Deliverance

Write down the names of your exes (if you are not married) and, one by one, release yourself from those soul ties. Say, for example, "Jason, I release you from your soul tie with me and I forgive you. I release myself from the soul tie that I have or had with you in Jesus name." If you are married, writing down the names of your exes could cause conflict, so pray with your husband and say, for example, "We release ourselves from every false covenant and soul tie that we are a part of, and we release the people who have tied themselves to us illegally."

ESTHER'S EDICT

Esther's Confession

I am free to love. I am not bound to any false covenant. I will not allow the wrong people to occupy spaces in my life that God has reserved for the right people. I am free from all ungodly soul ties. I will not harass, tempt or belittle any person who God has removed from my life. I call forward the people who God has assigned to my life. I am free to love them, honor them and understand them. I will be a blessing to them.

ESTHER TRACKER
(Month Eleven)

This is your journal for the month. List upcoming events, past incidents, your fears, your concerns, your expectations, your hopes, how you intend to respond to the issues you're facing, how you've responded to each issue/incident that you have faced (this month), and how you plan to improve so that you'll be a better woman next month.

If you need more space to write, please use a notebook, but be sure to get it all out.

Before you move on to the journal, please write a note/declaration to yourself (in the box below), detailing how you intend to manage this month.

Note to Self

Week One

Week Two

Week Three

Week Four

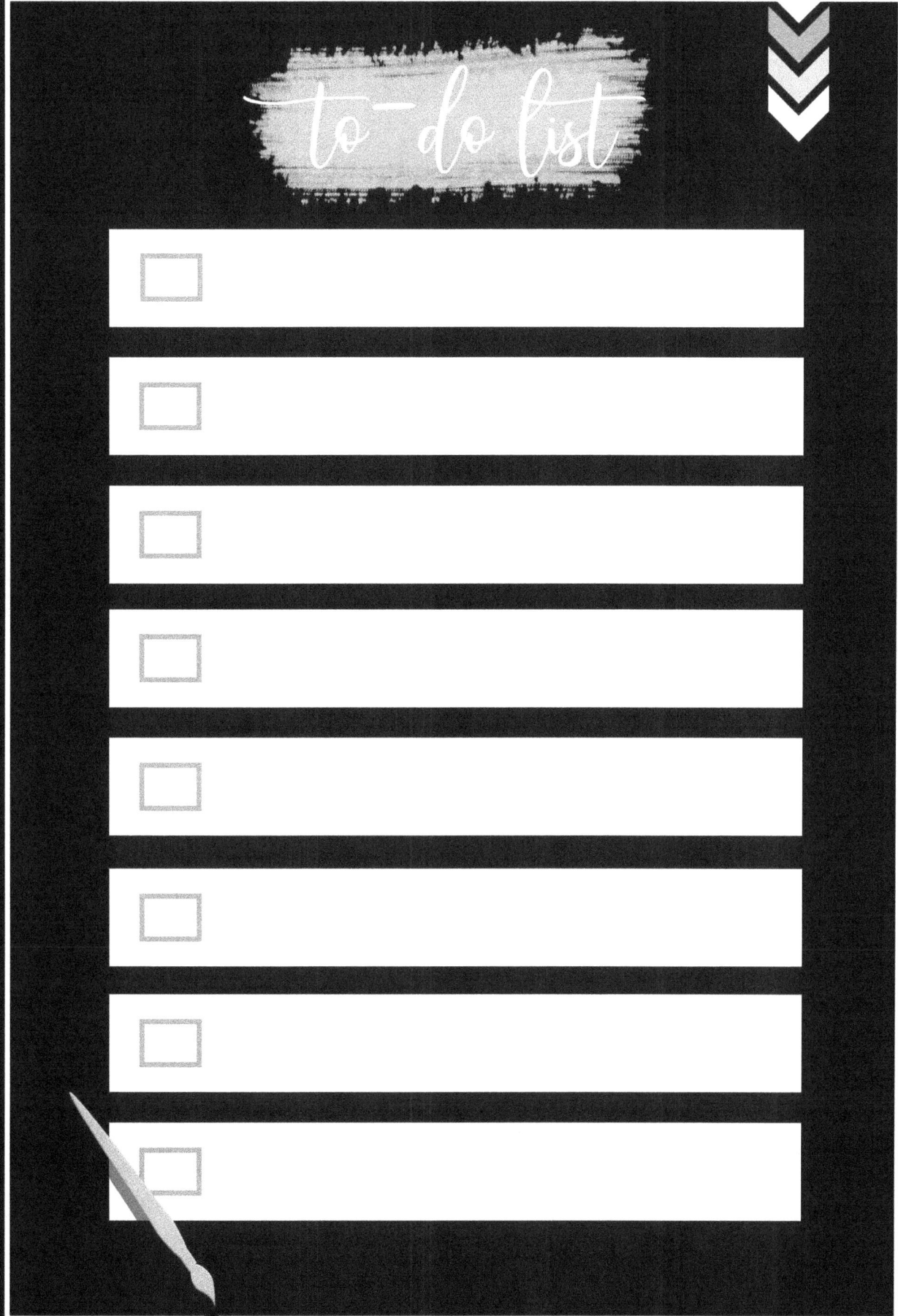

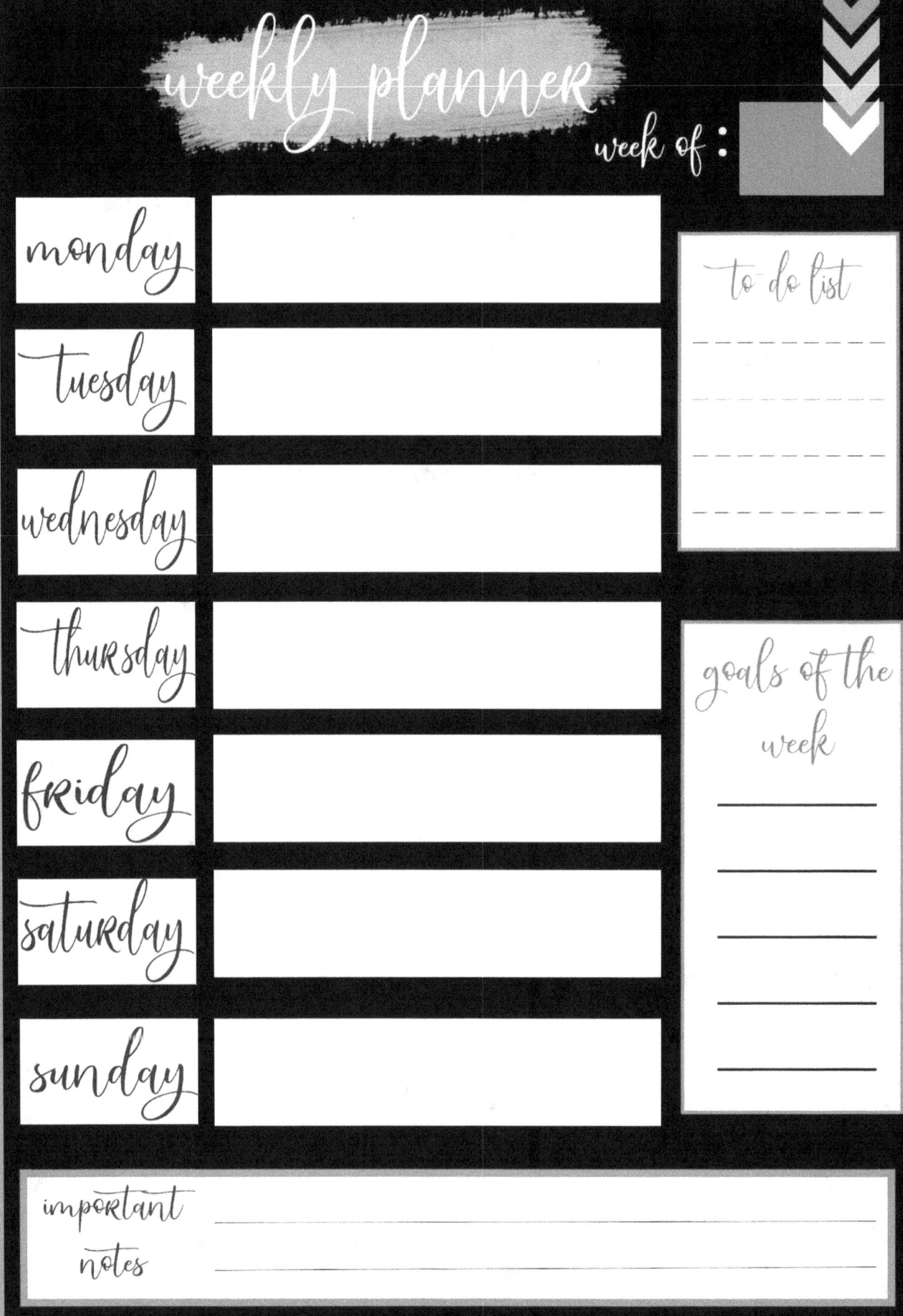

Month Twelve

Possess the Promise

CROWN JEWEL XII

Galatians 5:16-25 reads, "This I say then, Walk in the Spirit, and ye shall not fulfil the lust of the flesh. For the flesh lusteth against the Spirit, and the Spirit against the flesh: and these are contrary the one to the other: so that ye cannot do the things that ye would. But if ye be led of the Spirit, ye are not under the law. Now the works of the flesh are manifest, which are these; Adultery, fornication, uncleanness, lasciviousness, idolatry, witchcraft, hatred, variance, emulations, wrath, strife, seditions, heresies, envyings, murders, drunkenness, revellings, and such like: of the which I tell you before, as I have also told you in time past, that they which do such things shall not inherit the kingdom of God. But the fruit of the Spirit is love, joy, peace, longsuffering, gentleness, goodness, faith, meekness, temperance: against such there is no law. And they that are Christ's have crucified the flesh with the affections and lusts. If we live in the Spirit, let us also walk in the Spirit."

Esther had a closet. Whenever she woke up in the morning, she had to decide what she was going to wear. She knew that, like most days, her King was not going to summon her. Nevertheless, she had to look and behave like a Queen, even when she was surrounded by eunuchs, jealous women and people who hated the Jews. She had to look her best, even if she was going to her garden. Every move she made influenced another woman. Every word she spoke was echoed by the many women in the kingdom. But her closet wasn't just a huge room filled with gowns, robes and crowns, it was the thoughts that crowded or crowned her mind everyday. She had to choose between right and wrong, wrath and love, strife and peace—and get this, it wasn't always easy. but she'd been built for this! She'd been broken for this! And more than anything, she'd been born for this!

HEAVEN'S LOVE LETTER TO YOU

Dear Queen,
I want you to imagine a battle in the biblical days. Imagine the Israelites going up against the Jebusites in the now infamous war for the Promised Land. I want you to imagine Israel defeating their enemies, and then, once the war was over, returning to Egypt to settle down. Why would they do that? Why go through all of those wars and all of that warfare to finally possess the promise, only to return to the slimy pits of bondage that God dug them out of? Isn't this what many believers do today? They fight and they win, but many don't possess the promise. Why is this? Because, somehow in the heat of the battle, they've lost their ability to love others. Queen, out of all the catastrophes and losses you can suffer through, whatever you do, don't forget to guard your heart. Beautiful lady, please don't lose your love. What you have to do is put on the right attitude and then go and work in your garden. In that garden, you

have to uproot the works of the flesh and grow the fruits of the Spirit. And this isn't an easy task because there are many enemies from pests (demons) to storms (people) that will come against your harvest. Howbeit, if you fight your way through the tears, the persecution and the rejection, and you guard your heart along the way, your wisdom will grow alongside your faith. This is what qualifies you for the greatest crown any Queen could ever possess, and that is the crown of Love.

"So we have come to know and to believe the love that God has for us. God is love, and whoever abides in love abides in God, and God abides in him" (1 John 4:16).

PROVERBS 19:14

House and riches are the inheritance of fathers: and a prudent wife is from the LORD.

WHAT HAVE YOU LEARNED FROM THE SCRIPTURE AND VERSES ABOVE, AND HOW DO YOU PLAN TO APPLY WHAT YOU'VE LEARNED TO YOUR LIFE?

1	
2	
3	
4	
5	
6	
7	

8	
9	
10	
11	
12	
13	
14	
15	

ESTHER TRACER
(Month Twelve)

List your fears and other issues, trace them all the way to their roots, and then list what you're going to do to train them. How do you plan to get free? What books are you reading? Who's your therapist? What programs are you in? If you want to grow, heal and be delivered, you have to be intentional and consistent with monitoring and managing your mind.

List Each Fear/ Insecurity/ Issue	Trace Each Fear and Insecurity	Train Each Fear and Insecurity

ESTHER'S TRAIL

(Month Twelve)

Any time you participate in any of the events listed below, be sure to pencil in the date. Note, you can write as many dates into one window that you can fit into each space. The goal is to teach you to enjoy your own company.

Event	Dates	Event	Dates
Did Something Nice for Myself		Went to Church	
Dined in Restaurant		Studied Bible	
Exercised		Went to Church	
Encouraged Someone		Studied Bible	
Blessed Someone		Went to Church	
Overcame an Offense		Studied Bible	
Expressed Myself Creatively		Went to Church	
Resisted Temptation		Studied Bible	
Learned Something New		Went to Church	
Broke Cultural Barriers		Studied Bible	
Challenged Myself		Went to Church	

PRAYER CLOSET

Esther's Prayer

Dear Lord,

I ask that You give me the wisdom and the boldness to possess the promise. Dismantle all of my excuses. Open my eyes to my identity and assignment in You. Send me forward and give me the wisdom, tools and relationships I need to manifest my assignment in the Earth. Give me face-to-face encounters with You. Fill every inch of my mind and body with Your love and Your power, and use me for Your glory. Help me to retain every good lesson I've learned, and take away the pain, demonic residue and traumatic memories that would serve to plague and hinder me. Instead, help me to remember what You've done for me and not what others have done to me. Deliver me from procrastination. I am a willing vessel. Use me to glorify Your name.

It is in Jesus name that I pray,

Amen.

CHALLENGE OF THE MONTH

Esther's Deliverance

Send a text to all of the people in your life saying, "I love and appreciate you." Do NOT get offended if they don't respond. Some people are not good at expressing themselves; they hate to feel vulnerable. That's their issue; don't make it yours! Spend this month hugging and loving on people, expressing love everywhere you go. Remember this—there is healing power in your love. Share it with others; this is how you make it work for you!

ESTHER'S EDICT

Esther's Confession

I am not who I used to be. I am not who hurt caused me to become. I am beautifully and wonderfully made. I am an expression of God's love in the Earth.

ESTHER TRACKER
(Month Twelve)

This is your journal for the month. List upcoming events, past incidents, your fears, your concerns, your expectations, your hopes, how you intend to respond to the issues you're facing, how you've responded to each issue/incident that you have faced (this month), and how you plan to improve so that you'll be a better woman next month.

If you need more space to write, please use a notebook, but be sure to get it all out.

Before you move on to the journal, please write a note/declaration to yourself (in the box below), detailing how you intend to manage this month.

Note to Self

Week One

Week Two

Week Three

Week Four

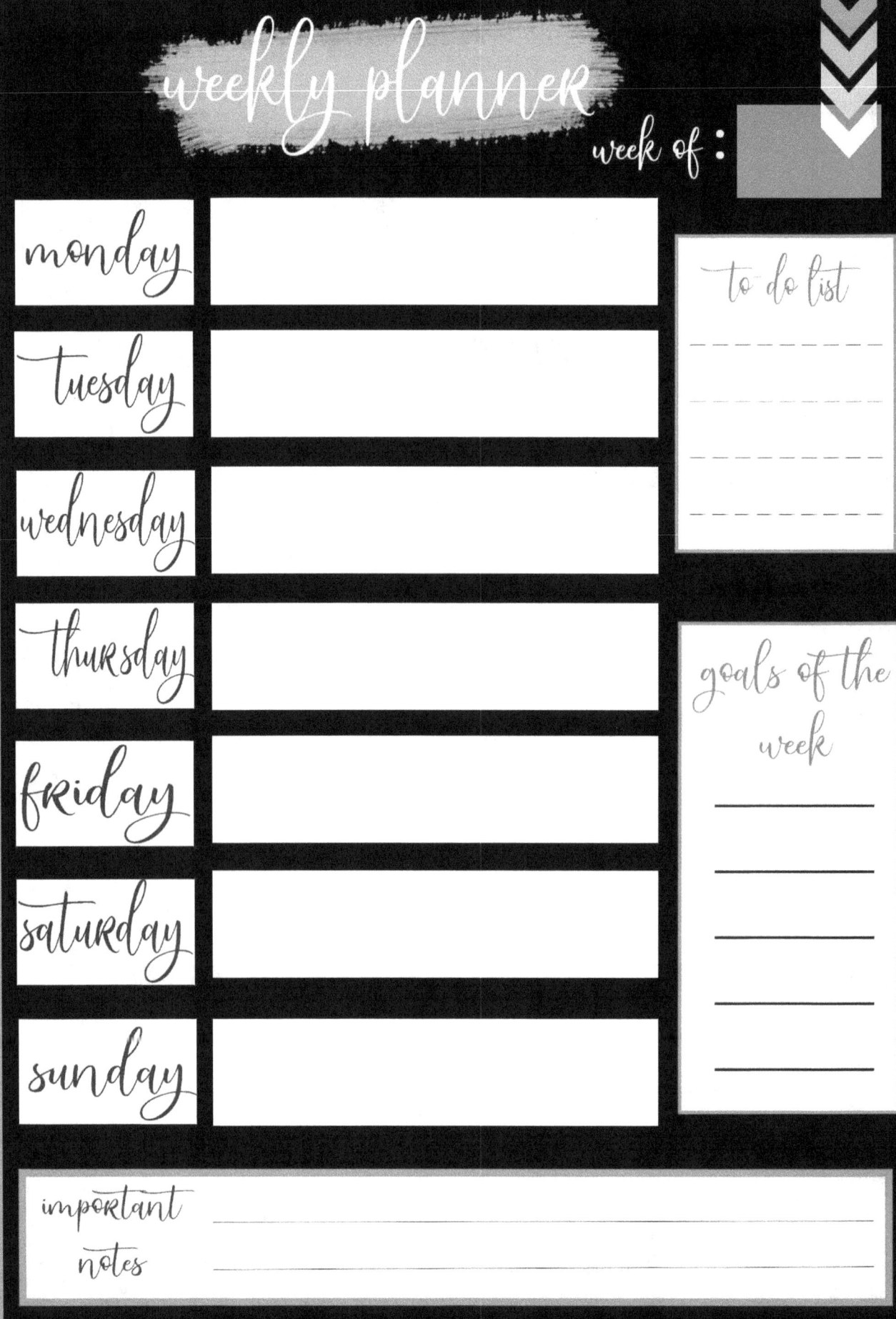

Personal Constitution

Established

How to Use the Constitution

The goal of a Constitution is to govern a body, whether that body be a government, a movement or a person. Your Personal Constitution is designed for you to govern yourself: mind, body and spirit. The average believer has no tool of self-governance. Consequently, most believers are led by their emotions. They sow the wrong seeds and reap harvests that are not fit for Kings and Queens. In truth, this is because most people have never been taught why it is important to write the vision, make it plain and manifest it.

Look at each section of your Personal Constitution and write down how you intend to govern yourself in each area. Remember, countries don't prepare for war in times of war; they prepare for war in times of peace. In other words, don't wait for Satan to attack you in a certain area before you start establishing rules, policies and boundaries. You can prevent an attack by setting order in each area of your life, and you can further secure and revise your rules whenever that area of your life is tested or attacked. This is what governments and businesses do. This is how they become stronger, wiser and more secure. This is also how they become wealthier.

Look at the following example to better understand how to use the Personal Constitution.

SECTION	DECLARATION
Temple/Physical Body	I will present my body as a living sacrifice, holy and acceptable to God. In other words, I will not fornicate or practice any form of sexual immorality. In addition, I will not eat foods high in cholesterol and fat. I will limit my calorie intake to 2500 calories a day.
Mind/Mental Health	I will guard my heart. I will not listen to music that advises me against the Word of God. I will guard my ears and my tongue. I will not listen to or participate in gossip or slander. I will guard my peace. I will not maintain close relationships with toxic people. Instead, I will love them from a distance, but I will be there to stand in the gap for them whenever they need me.
Soul/Spirit	I will pray at least twice a day for thirty minutes or more each interval. I will study my Bible at least once a day. I will attend church at least once a week.

Dates and Definitions

The following definitions were taken from Google.

- Article: a piece of writing included with others in a newspaper, magazine, or other publication.
- Ratify: sign or give formal consent to (a treaty, contract, or agreement), making it officially valid.
- Amendment: a minor change or addition designed to improve a text, piece of legislation, etc.
- Section: any of the more or less distinct parts into which something is or may be divided or from which it is made up; a distinct group within a larger body of people or things.
- Repeal: revoke or annul; the action of revoking or annulling a law or congressional act.

First line shows an example of how to use the chart below.

Event	Dates	Action	Event	Date	Action
Relationship	08/24/20	Amended	Relationship	08/29/20	Repealed

Event	Dates	Action	Event	Date	Action

UNDERSTANDING LEGALITIES

God, throughout the scriptures, identified Himself as "I Am." This is in direct correlation to Isaiah 55:11, which reads, "So shall my word be that goeth forth out of my mouth: it shall not return unto me void, but it shall accomplish that which I please, and it shall prosper in the thing whereto I sent it" and Hebrews 16:18, which says, "That by two immutable things, in which it was impossible for God to lie, we might have a strong consolation, who have fled for refuge to lay hold upon the hope set before us." What this means is that whenever God speaks, whatever He says has no choice but to come to pass. This is why it is impossible for Him to tell a lie. He is the Word and the Word is Him. If God looked at the blue sky and said that it was red, He wouldn't be lying because the moment He spoke those words, the sky would immediately turn red. Everything, both small and great, must obey Him unless He gives it "will." And even then, there is a consequence to disobedience. So, when God refers to Himself as "I Am," everything that follows that statement is truth because He is the Truth. He embodies His Word because He is His Word.

We were created in the image and likeness of God, and amazingly enough, the majority of us are completely oblivious to the power of our words. When we say, "I am," whatever we say after that (legally) attaches itself to us. So, if someone says, "I am sad," or "I am sick," that person is attaching sadness and sickness to himself or herself. While the feelings may be facts, they aren't truths. What's the difference? A fact is temporal. It is what man can establish and produce sufficient evidence to support. It's what we can see, taste, touch, hear or smell. The wind is a fact; even though we can't see it, we can feel and sometimes hear it. The clouds are facts; even though we can't touch them, we can see them. The more tangible something is, the easier it is to prove it to be a fact. For example, a flower is a fact because we can see, smell, touch and taste it, even though we can't necessarily hear it. The truth, on the other hand, is the Word of God. So, for example, while you may "feel" sick, the truth is "But he was wounded for our transgressions, he was bruised for our iniquities: the chastisement of our peace was upon him; and with his stripes we are healed" (Isaiah 53:5). Howbeit, whatever we bind on Earth is bound in Heaven, whatever we loose on Earth is loosed in Heaven (see Matthew 18:18). When we say "I am," we are speaking of our identity, therefore, when we attach a word, phrase or condition to our identities, we immediately become what we say. But what if you do feel sick? What if the doctor diagnosed you with some sort of ailment? The disease may be a fact, but it's not the truth. So, the better way to respond is to say, "I feel sick," instead of "I am sick." It is always good practice to follow up the statement with the truth. In other words, simply quote scriptures about healing. This isn't to get the disease to "go away," since you can't divorce what you agree with. The goal is to get your mind to fall out of agreement with the disease. This happens through knowledge (information), understanding (processing that information) and wisdom (correctly applying that information). This causes you to go wholeheartedly into agreement with God, and when this happens, miracles are inevitable. Healing has to manifest itself because the Truth cannot return to the Lord void. "Jesus saith unto him, I am the way, the truth, and the life: no man cometh unto the Father, but by me" (John 14:6).

Another legal statement that God makes is, "I will." For example, in John 14:18, He said, "I will not leave you comfortless: I will come to you." This is prophetic language, and while it is futuristic to us, it is still a present Truth. Once this event finally comes to pass, it manifests itself in the realm of the Earth as a fact, meaning, we can now use our sensory organs to see, hear, smell, touch or taste it.

And finally, God often said throughout the scriptures, "Thou shall" or "Thou shalt not." Of course, this simply means, "You should" or "You should not," but the word "should" is not suggestive language. In other words, God is giving a command, but because we have "will," or better yet the ability to choose right or wrong, we have rendered the word "should" to be suggestive. What we have to do is agree with God by saying, "I will" or "I will not," and of course, these words must be followed up with an action (obedience). When God says, "Thou shalt not," but we do contrary to what He's spoken, we enter an event called rebellion, which the scriptures tell us is as the sin of witchcraft. The goal is to fully agree with God; this is how we walk alongside Him. Amos 3:3 says it this way, "Can two walk together, except they be agreed?"

What's the point of all this? To get you to understand the power of your words! So, when you say in your Personal Constitution, for example, I will not have sex outside of marriage, what you're doing is making a legal decree. In other words, what you are doing is agreeing with God and making your stance known. Get this—God is not going to hover over your words to catch you in a lie. Instead, should you fail, His love will cover a multitude of your sins and His grace will be sufficient for you. This doesn't give us a license to sin (grace is not a condom), it's simply a part of our insurance package should we fall into sin. Making a legal decree and publicizing it makes you less likely to fall into error because it becomes more than an emotionally-driven statement; this is why God told Habakkuk, "Write the vision and make it plain on tablets" (Habakkuk 2:2). This is also why He published the Ten Commandments on two stone tablets.

With that said, use the Personal Constitution to set order in your life. Pray over them; ask the Holy Spirit to assist you with honoring your decrees.

The Constitution of

Your Name
Established

/ /

Self Declaration

SELF-GOVERNANCE

ARTICLE I

SECTION	DECLARATION
Temple/Physical Body	
Mind/Mental Health	
Soul/Spirit	

AMENDMENTS	DECLARATION

Familial Relationships

Article II

Section	Declaration
Offense	
Boundaries	
Money/Loans/Repayments	
Conversations	
Visitations	
My Children	
Scriptures	

Amendments	Declaration

Platonic Relationships

Article III

Section	Declaration
Offense	
Boundaries	
Money/Loans/Repayments	
Conversations	
Visitations	
My Children	
Scriptures	

Amendments	Declaration

Romantic Relationships

Article IV

Section	Declaration
Offense	
Boundaries	
Money/Loans/Repayments	
Conversations	
Visitations	
My Children	
Scriptures	

Amendments	Declaration

Money Matters

Article V

Section	Declaration
Debt (Repayment)	
Boundaries (Spending)	
Investments	
Allowances	
Charitie	
My Children	
Scriptures	

Amendments	Declaration

Peer/Professional Relationships

Article VI

Section	Declaration
Offense	
Boundaries	
Money/Loans/Repayments	
Conversations	
Visitations	
My Children	
Scriptures	

Amendments	Declaration

Other Relationships

Article VII

Section	Declaration
Offense	
Boundaries	
Money/Loans/Repayments	
Conversations	
Visitations	
My Children	
Scriptures	

Amendments	Declaration

Queens & Things

Deliverance
Legality
Royalty
Vashti
Prince
Court
Noble
Lord

Honorable
Princess
Lavish
Esther
Tiara
Crown
Jews
King

Dignified
Victory
Xerxes
Castle
Staff
Jesus
Pink
Hero

Anointed
Kingdom
Throne
Pretty
Queen
Regal
Love

www.ingramcontent.com/pod-product-compliance
Lightning Source LLC
Chambersburg PA
CBHW080439170426
43195CB00017B/2822